Mile by Mile

ON THE L.M.S.

by

S. N. PIKE, M.B.E.

MIDLAND REGION EDITION
BRITISH RAILWAYS

The journey between Euston and St. Pancras and the North and North-West described in detail :—

- GRADIENTS OF THE LINE
- SPEED TESTS AND MILEAGES
- VIADUCTS, BRIDGES AND EMBANKMENTS
- TUNNELS, CUTTINGS AND CROSSOVERS
- STREAMS, RIVERS AND ROADS
- MINES, FACTORIES AND WORKS

with an account of features of interest and beauty to be seen from the train.

A facsimile reprint by

Silver Link Publishing Ltd
Unit 5, Home Farm Close, Church Street,
Wadenhoe, Peterborough PE8 5TE

1

© Nick Dodson 1988

Originally published in 1947 by Stuart N. Pike, Worthing
Facsimile edition first published in December 1988
by Silver Link Publishing Ltd
Reprinted March 1993

British Library Cataloguing in Publication Data

Pike, S. N. (Stuart N)
Mile by mile on the LMS.
I. Title
385.0941

ISBN 0 947971 90 4

Printed and bound in Great Britain

Author's Note

In this, my third railway book, I have to again acknowledge, with grateful thanks, the valuable assistance I have received from all grades of railway officials. Those whose daily work it is to ensure speedy and comfortable travel on the Midland Region of British Railways have thrown themselves enthusiastically into the task of helping me with the construction of this little book.

Embodied in this edition are many helpful suggestions received from readers of my previous books " Mile by Mile on the Southern Railway" and " Mile by Mile on the L.N.E.R." To these correspondents I am extremely grateful, and if I have not adopted all the ideas put forward it is because I wished to keep all three booklets in line as to style, size and price, so that they all may be considered as companion editions and, with the forthcoming Western Region edition (G.W. Railway), form a set covering the most used main railway lines in the country.

I am indebted to the Railway Publishing Co. Ltd. for their kind permission to reproduce certain of the diagrams from their publication " Gradients of British Main Line Railways."

To save correspondence I would say here that I will advise all old and new post customers for my books when the G.W. Railway (Western Region) edition is ready for sale, and as other railway books by me become available.

3 Canterbury House,   S. N. P.
    Worthing, Sussex.

Index to Stations

	Page		Page		Page
ACTON BRIDGE	36	GEDDINGTON	19	OAKHAM	19
ALFRETON	15	GLENDON	11	OAKLEY	10
ALLERTON	37	GREAT BRIDGEFORD	34	OLD DALBY	20
ALTOFTS	18	GREAT GLEN	12		
AMBERGATE	22	GREAT LONGSTONE	23	PARK GATE	16
AMPTHILL	9	GRETTON	19	PEAK FOREST	24
APSLEY	27	GRIMSTON	20	PLUMTREE	21
ARMITAGE	33			POLESWORTH	32
ASHWELL	20			PYE BRIDGE	14
ATHERSTONE	32	HALEBANK	37		
ATTERCLIFFE ROAD	16	HARLINGTON	9		
		HARPENDEN	8	RADFORD	21
		HARRINGWORTH	19	RADLETT	7
		HARROW	26	ROADE	29
BAKEWELL	23	HARTFORD	36	ROTHERHAM	16
BARROW-ON-SOAR	13	HATCH END	26	ROWSLEY	23
BEAUCHIEF	16	HATHERN	13	ROYSTON	17
BEDFORD	**10**	HEATON MERSEY	25	**RUGBY**	**31**
BELPER	22	HEELEY	16	RUGELEY	33
BERKHAMSTED	27	HEMEL HEMPSTED	27	RUNCORN	37
BLETCHLEY	**28**	HENDON	7		
BLISWORTH	29	HOLME	16	ST. ALBANS	8
BRIGHTSIDE	16	HUNSLET	18	SANDAL	17
BRINKLOW	31			SAXBY	20
BURTON LATIMER	11			SEFTON PARK	37
BUSHEY	26	ILKESTON JUNCTION	14	SHARNBROOK	10
BUXTON	24	IRCHESTER	10	SHEEPBRIDGE	15
BUXWORTH	24			**SHEFFIELD**	**16**
				SHILTON	31
		KEGWORTH	13	SHIPLEY GATE	14
CASTLETHORPE	29	KETTERING	11	SILEBY	13
CHAPEL-EN-LE-FRITH	24	KIBWORTH	12	**ST. PANCRAS**	**7**
CHEADLE HEATH	25	KILNHURST	16	SPONDON	22
CHEDDINGTON	28	KINGS LANGLEY	27	**STAFFORD**	**34**
CHESTERFIELD	**15**			STANDON BRIDGE	34
CHILTERN GREEN	8	LANGLEY MILL	14	STANTON GATE	14
CHINLEY	24	LEAGRAVE	8	STAPLEFORD	14
CHORLTON-CUM-HARDY	25	**LEEDS**	**18**	SWINTON	17
CLAY CROSS	15	**LEICESTER**	**12**	SYSTON	13
CODNOR PARK	14	LEIGHTON BUZZARD	28		
COLWICK	33	LICHFIELD	33	TAMWORTH	32
CORBY	19	**LIVERPOOL**	**37**	TRENT	14
COVENTRY	**31**	LONG EATON	14	TRING	27
CREWE	**35**	**LOUGHBOROUGH**	**13**	TROWELL	14
CRICKLEWOOD	7	LUTON	8		
CROMFORD	23			UNSTONE	15
CUDWORTH	17	MADELEY	35	UPPER BROUGHTON	21
		MANCHESTER	**25**	UPPINGHAM	19
		MANTON	19		
DARFIELD	17	MARKET HARBOROUGH	11	**WAKEFIELD**	**18**
DARLEY DALE	23	MATLOCK	23	WATFORD	26
DERBY	**22**	MATLOCK BATH	23	WATH-ON-DEARNE	17
DESBOROUGH	11	MELTON MOWBRAY	20	WAVERTREE	37
DIDSBURY	25	METHLEY	18	WEEDON	30
DITTON JUNCTION	37	MILFORD	33	**WELLINGBOROUGH**	**10**
DOE HILL	15	MILLERS DALE	23	WELTON	30
DORE	16	MILL HILL	7	WEMBLEY	26
DRONFIELD	16	MILLHOUSES	16	WEST ALLERTON	37
DUFFIELD	22	MONSAL DALE	23	WESTHOUSES	15
		MOSSLEY HILL	37	WHATSTANDWELL	22
				WHISSENDINE	20
EAST LANGTON	12	NAPSBURY	8	WHITMORE	35
EDGE HILL	37	NORMANTON	18	WIDMERPOOL	21
ELSTREE	7	**NORTHAMPTON**	**29**	WIGSTON	12
EUSTON	**26**	NORTON BRIDGE	34	WILLESDEN	26
		NOTTINGHAM	**21**	WINCOBANK	16
FLITWICK	9	NUNEATON	31	WINSFORD	36
				WITHINGTON	25
				WOLVERTON	**29**
				WOODLESFORD	18

Rivers we meet

	Page		Page
Aire	18	Meece Brook	34
Anker	32	Mersey	25, 37
Avon	31		
		Nene	10, 30
Bradford	23		
Brent	26	Ouse	10, 29
Bulbourne	27	Ouzle	28
Calder	18	Penk	34
Chater	19		
Colne	26	Rother	15
Derwent	14, 22, 23	Sence	12
Dove	17	Soar	13, 14
Dron	15	Sow	34
Ecclesbourne	22	Tame	32, 33
Erewash	14	Tove	29
Eye	20	Trent	21, 33
Gade	27	Ver	8
Gwash	19		
		Weaver	35/37
Ise	11	Welland	19
		Wreak	13, 20
Lea	8, 9		

Canals

	Page
Aire and Calder Canal	18
Ashby de la Zouch Canal	31
Coventry Canal	31/33
Cromford Canal	14, 22
Grand Union Canal	7, 12/14, 26/30
Grantham Canal	21
Manchester Ship Canal	37
Nutbrook Canal	14
Oxford Canal	30, 31
Shropshire Union Canal	36
Staffs. and Worcs. Canal	34
Trent and Mersey Canal	33, 36
Weaver Canal	37

For index of Tunnels and Water-Troughs en route see page 6

Tunnels en Route

			PAGE			PAGE
PRIMROSE HILL		1220 yds.	26	CORBY	1920 yds.	19
KENSAL GREEN		317 yds.	26	SEATON	203 yds.	19
WATFORD	1M.	57 yds.	27	GLASTON	1840 yds.	19
NORTHCHURCH		347 yds.	27	WING	305 yds.	19
LINSLADE		283 yds.	28	MANTON	746 yds.	19
STOWEHILL		492 yds.	30	ASFORDBY	419 yds.	20
KILSBY	1M.	666 yds.	30	SAXELBY	543 yds.	20
SHUGBOROUGH		770 yds.	33	GRIMSTON	1305 yds.	20
				STANTON	1330 yds.	21

BELSIZE	1M.	66 yds.	7	MILFORD		853 yds.	22
ELSTREE		1050 yds.	7	AMBERGATE		101 yds.	22
AMPTHILL		718 yds.	9	WHATSTANDWELL		149 yds.	22
KNIGHTON		104 yds.	12	LEA WOOD		315 yds.	22
ALFRETON		840 yds.	15	WILLERSLEY		746 yds.	23
BROOMHOUSE		92 yds.	15	HIGH TOR		755 yds.	23
BRADWAY	1M.	267 yds	16	HADDON		1058 yds.	23
				CRESSBROOK		471 yds.	23
				LITTON		515 yds.	23
				CHEE TOR		616 yds.	24
				GREAT ROCKS		100 yds.	24
				DOVE HOLES	1M.	1224 yds.	24
				DISLEY	2M.	346 yds.	24

Water-Trough Installations en Route

BUSHEY TROUGHS	MILEPOST 16	PAGE 26
CASTLETHORPE TROUGHS	MILEPOST 54	PAGE 29
RUGBY TROUGHS	MILEPOST 84	PAGE 31
HADEMORE TROUGHS	MILEPOST 114	PAGE 33
WHITMORE TROUGHS	MILEPOST 148	PAGE 35
HALEBANK TROUGHS	MILEPOST 184	PAGE 37

OAKLEY TROUGHS	MILEPOST 54	PAGE 10
LOUGHBOROUGH TROUGHS	MILEPOST 112	PAGE 13

MELTON TROUGHS	MILEPOST 104	PAGE 20

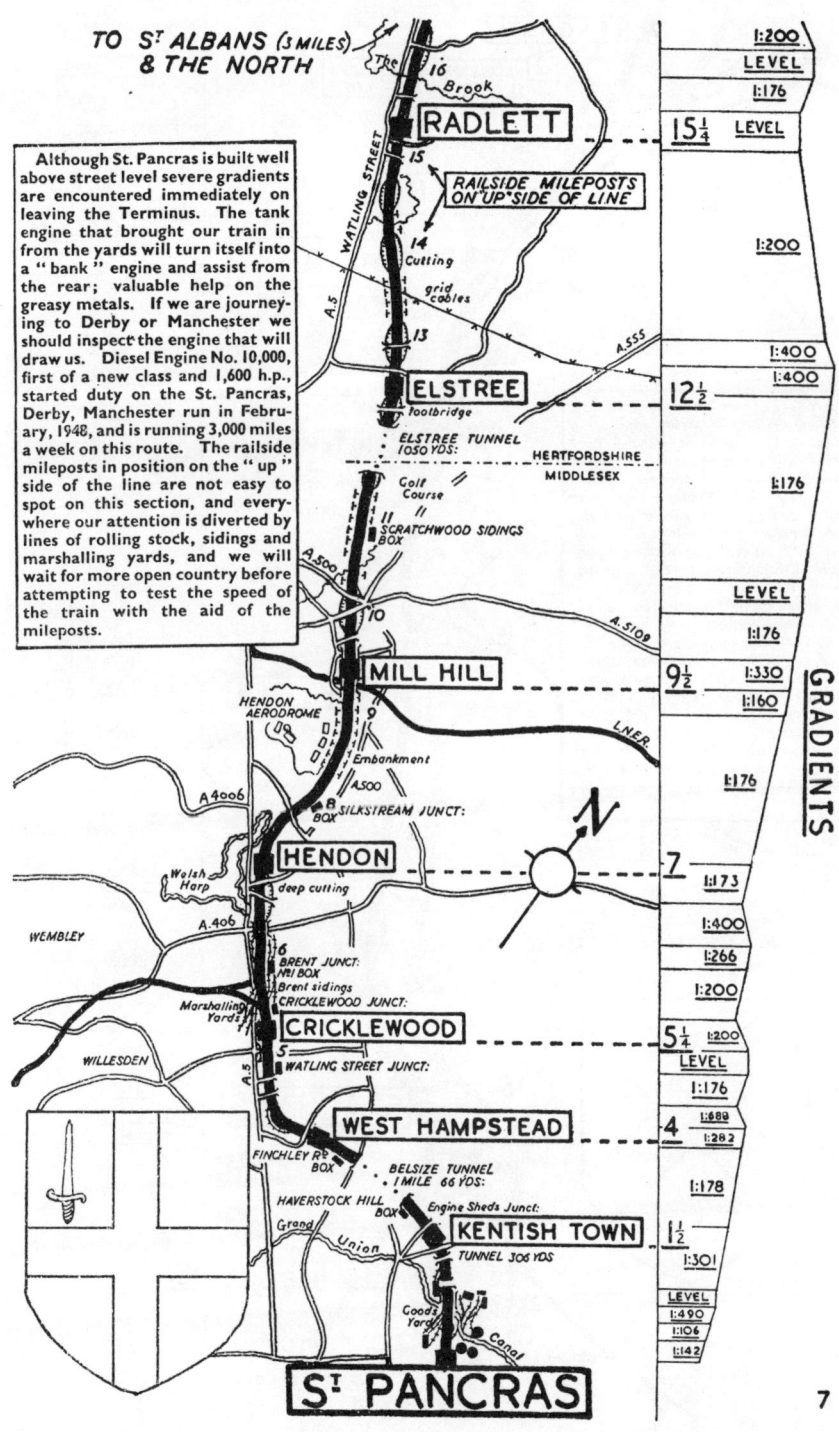

Although St. Pancras is built well above street level severe gradients are encountered immediately on leaving the Terminus. The tank engine that brought our train in from the yards will turn itself into a "bank" engine and assist from the rear; valuable help on the greasy metals. If we are journeying to Derby or Manchester we should inspect the engine that will draw us. Diesel Engine No. 10,000, first of a new class and 1,600 h.p., started duty on the St. Pancras, Derby, Manchester run in February, 1948, and is running 3,000 miles a week on this route. The railside mileposts in position on the "up" side of the line are not easy to spot on this section, and everywhere our attention is diverted by lines of rolling stock, sidings and marshalling yards, and we will wait for more open country before attempting to test the speed of the train with the aid of the mileposts.

7

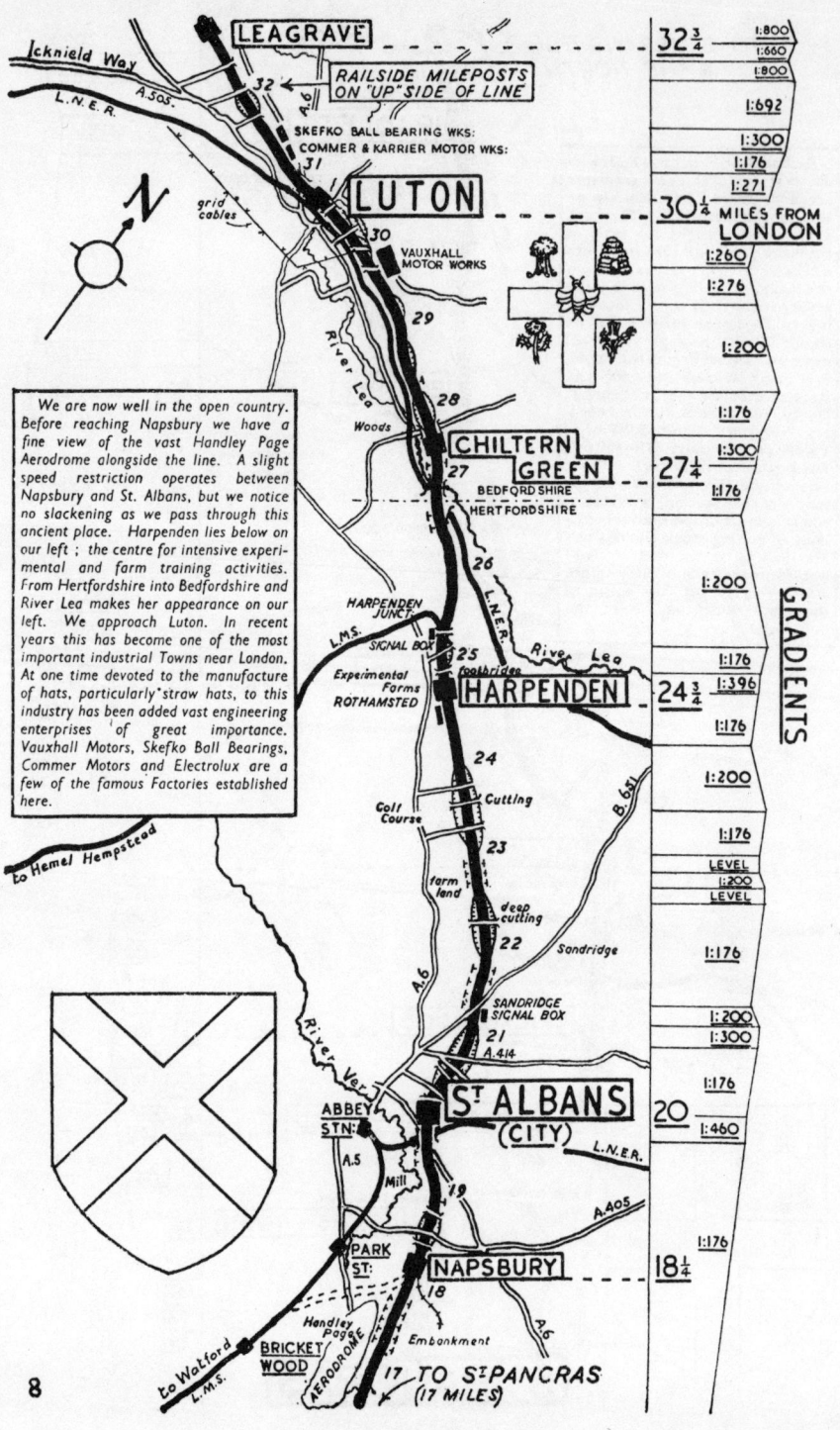

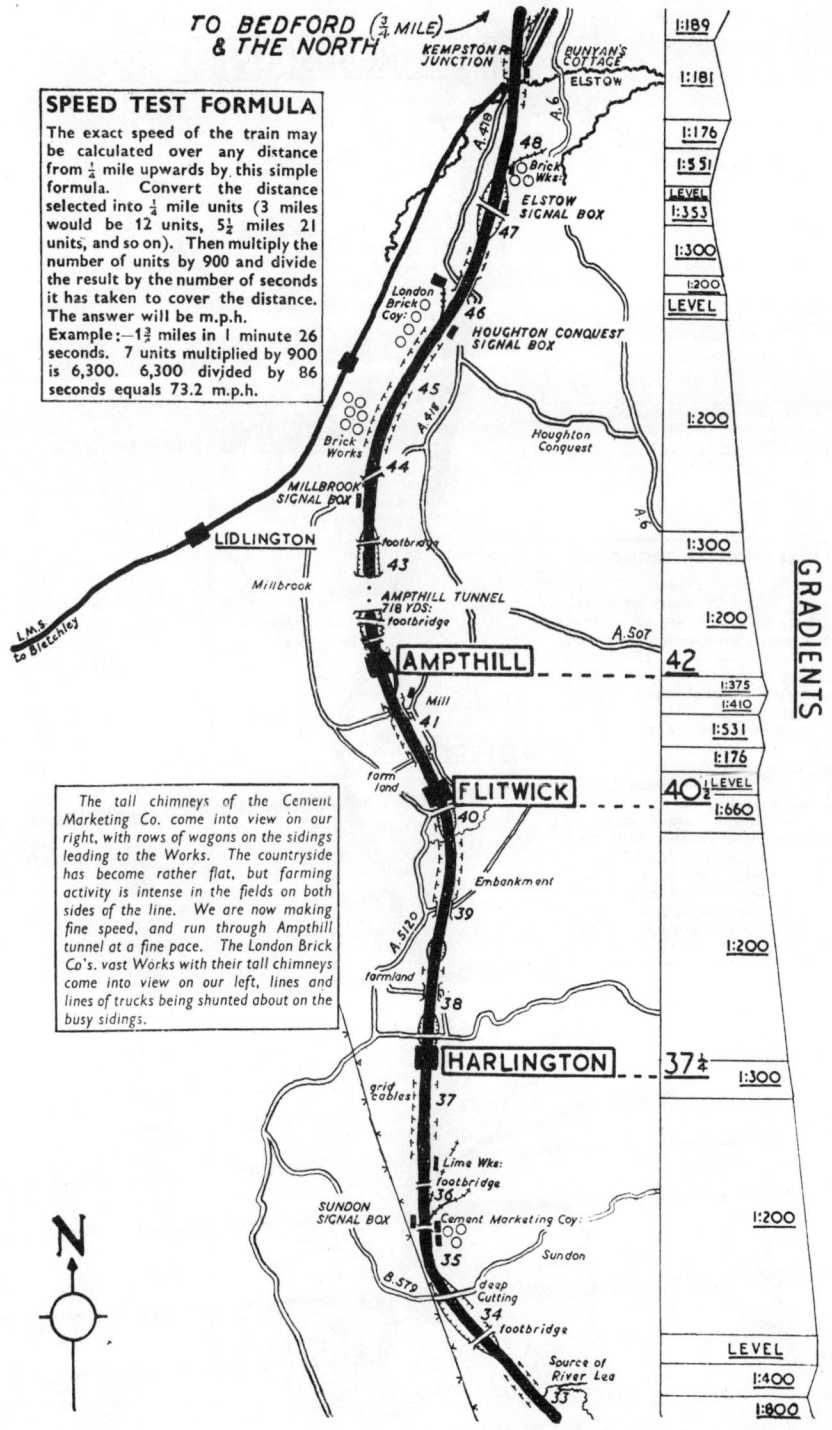

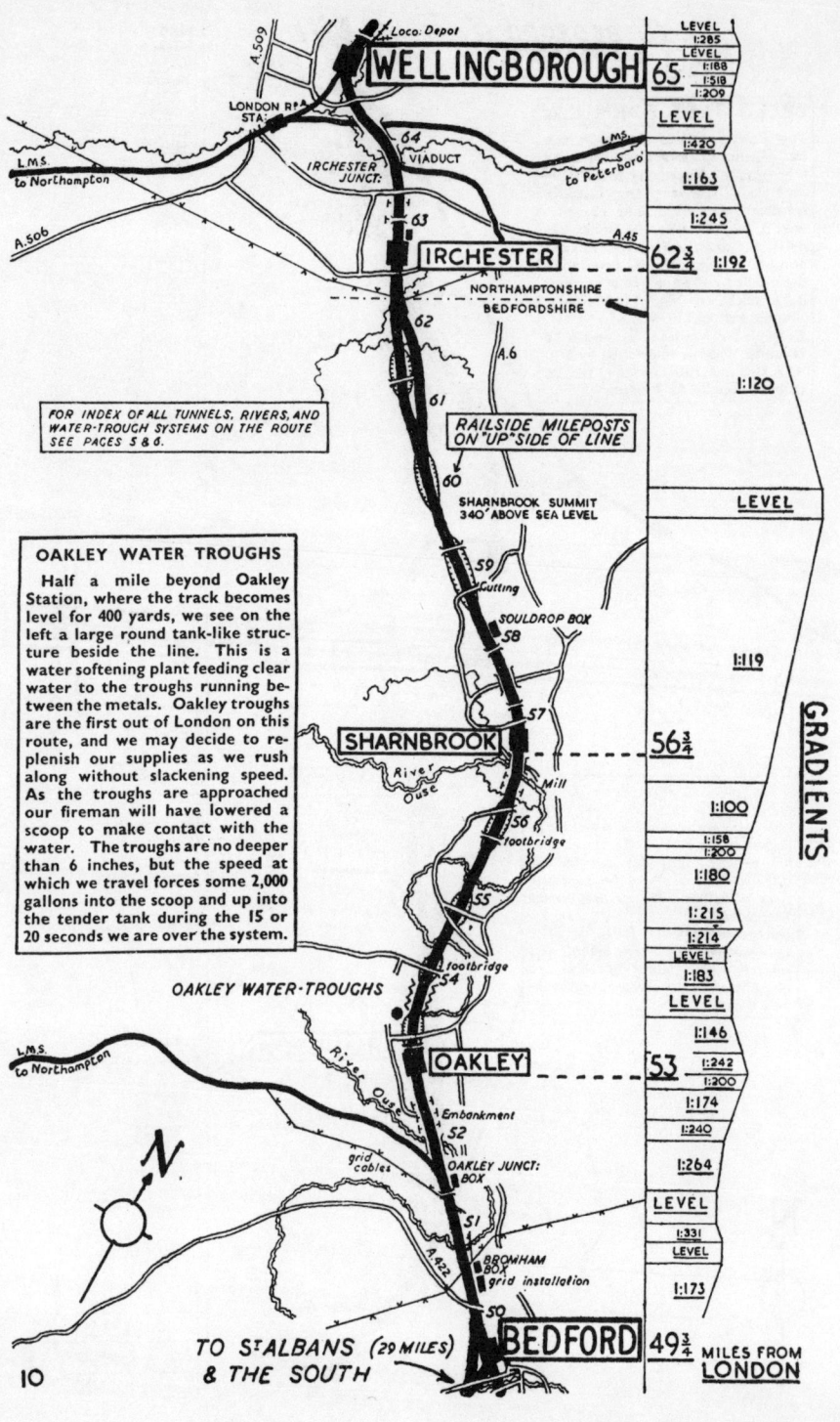

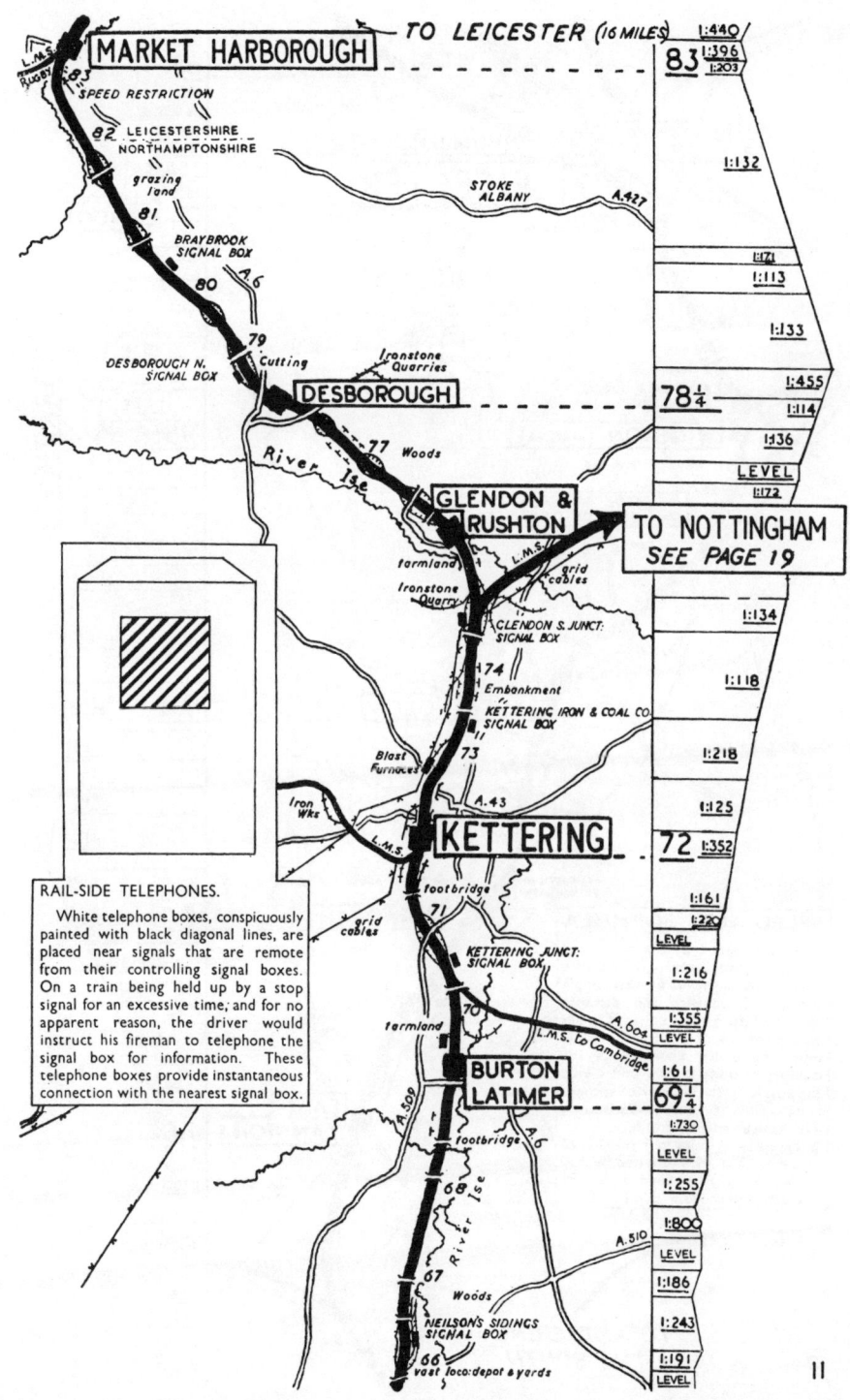

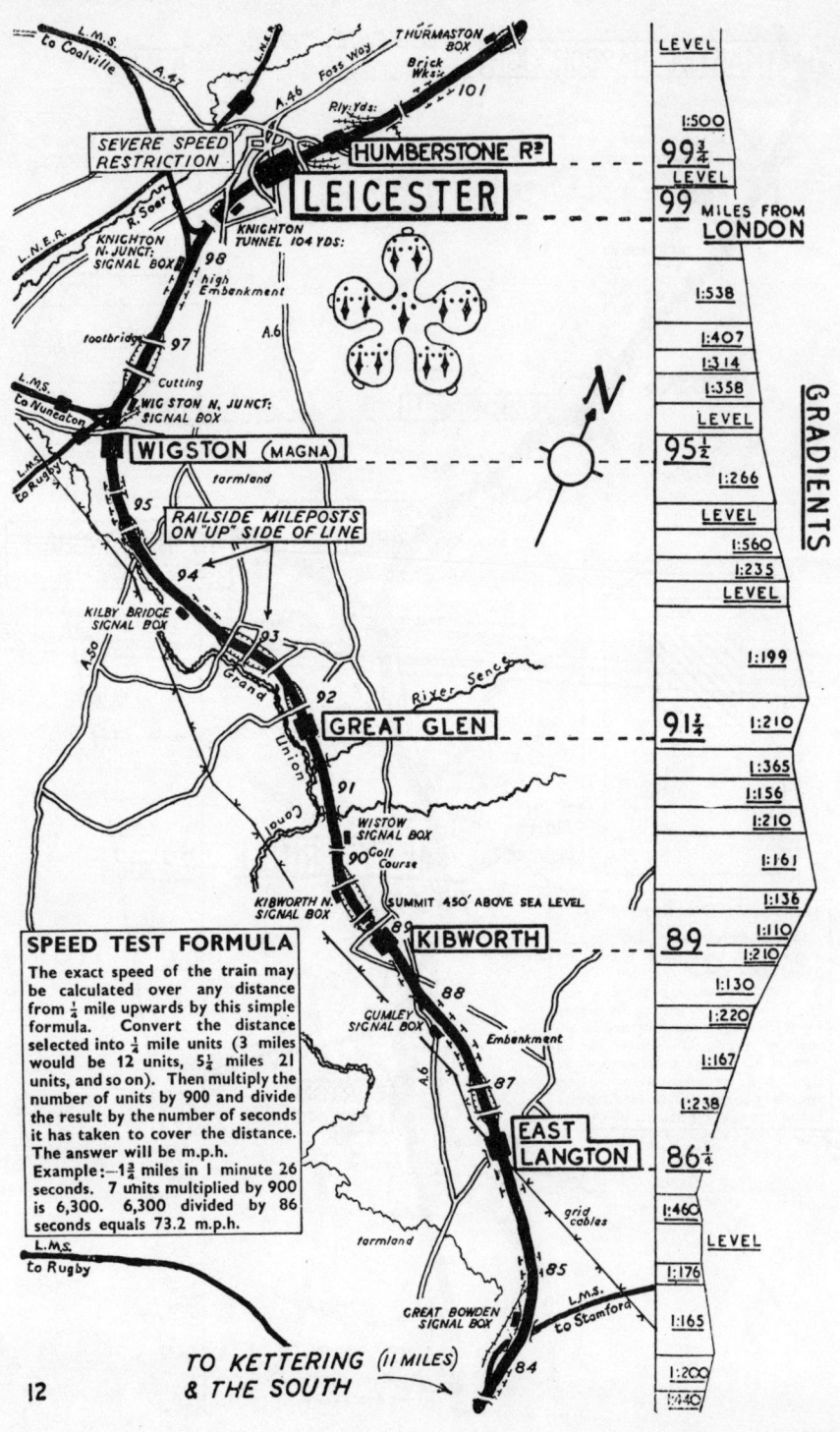

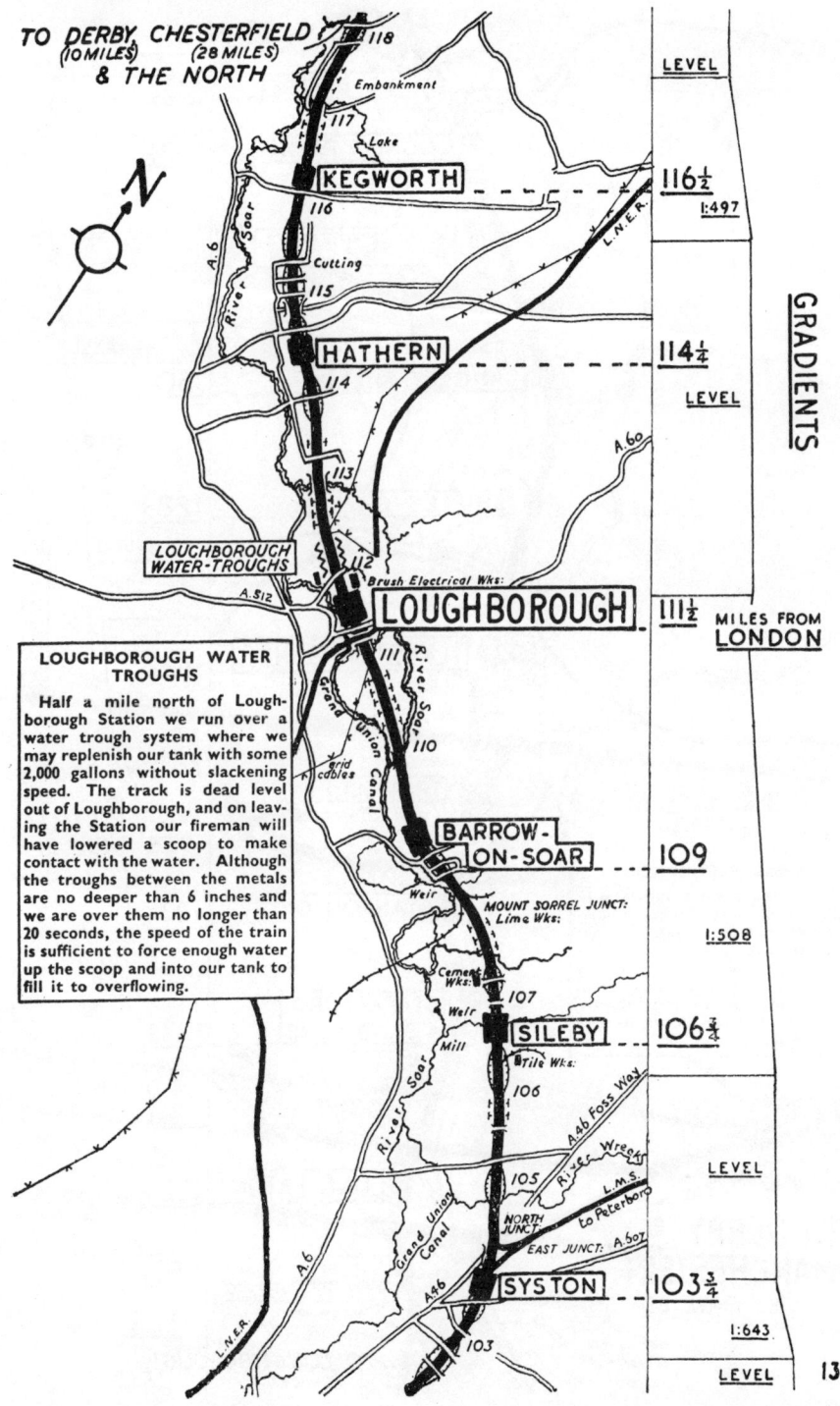

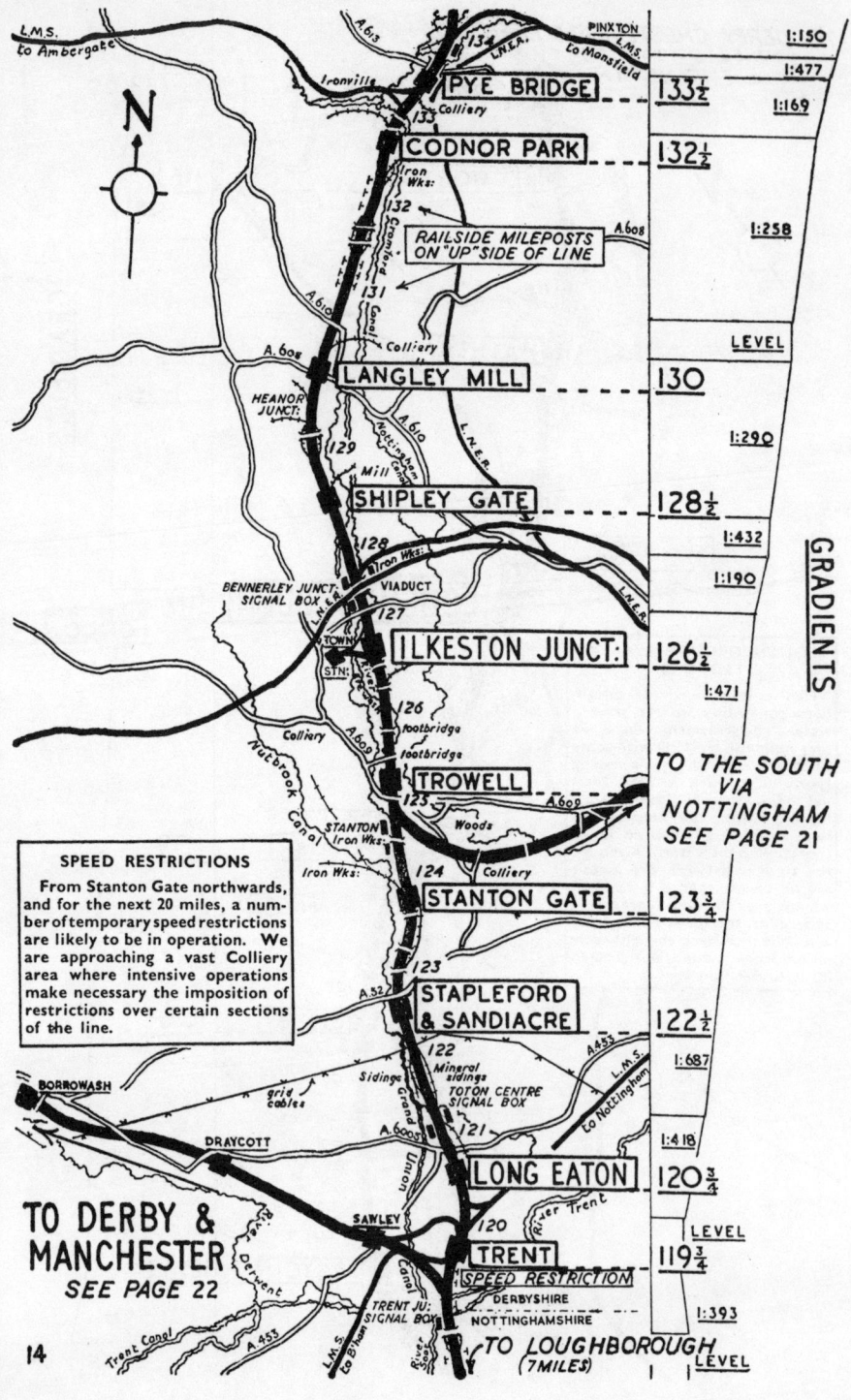

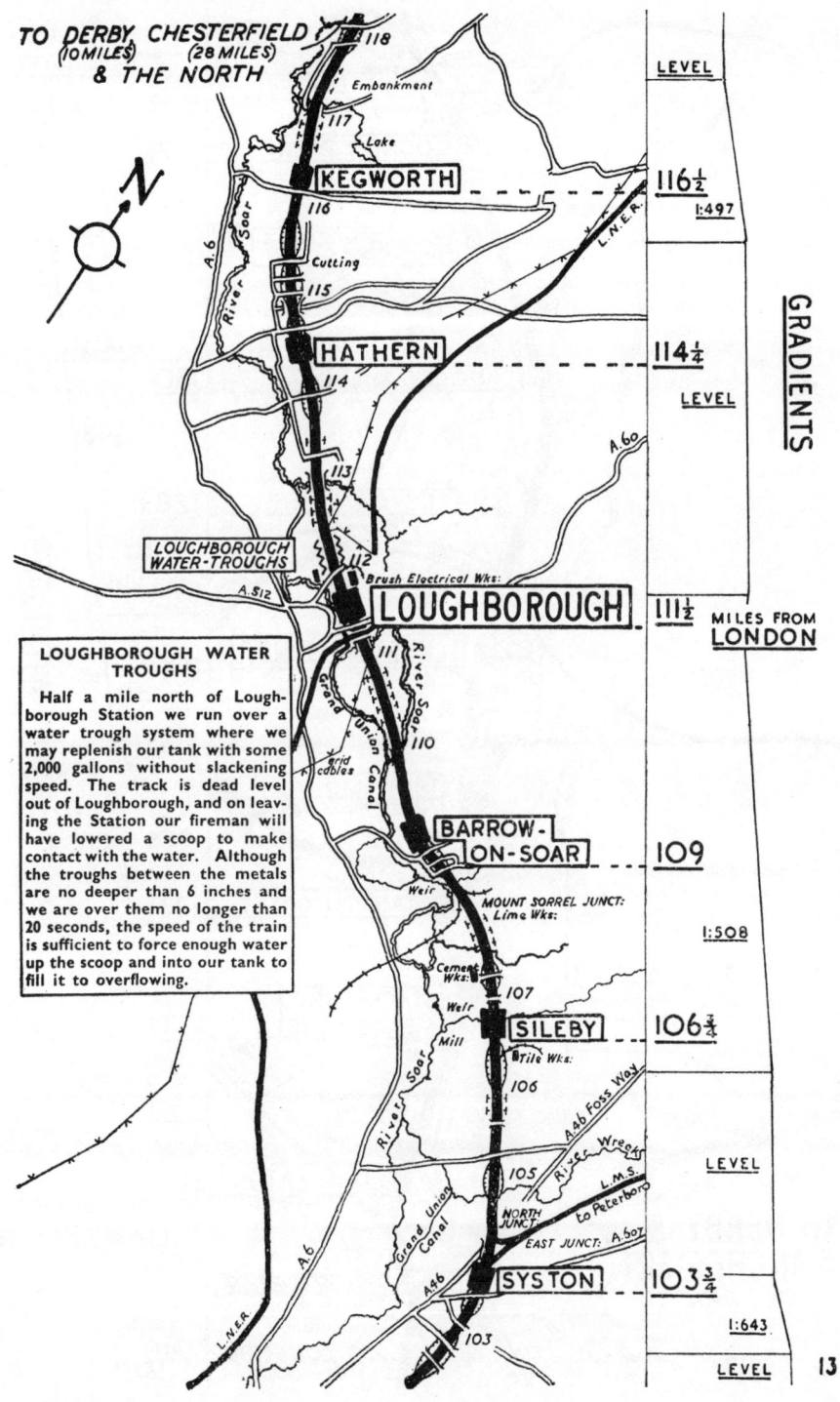

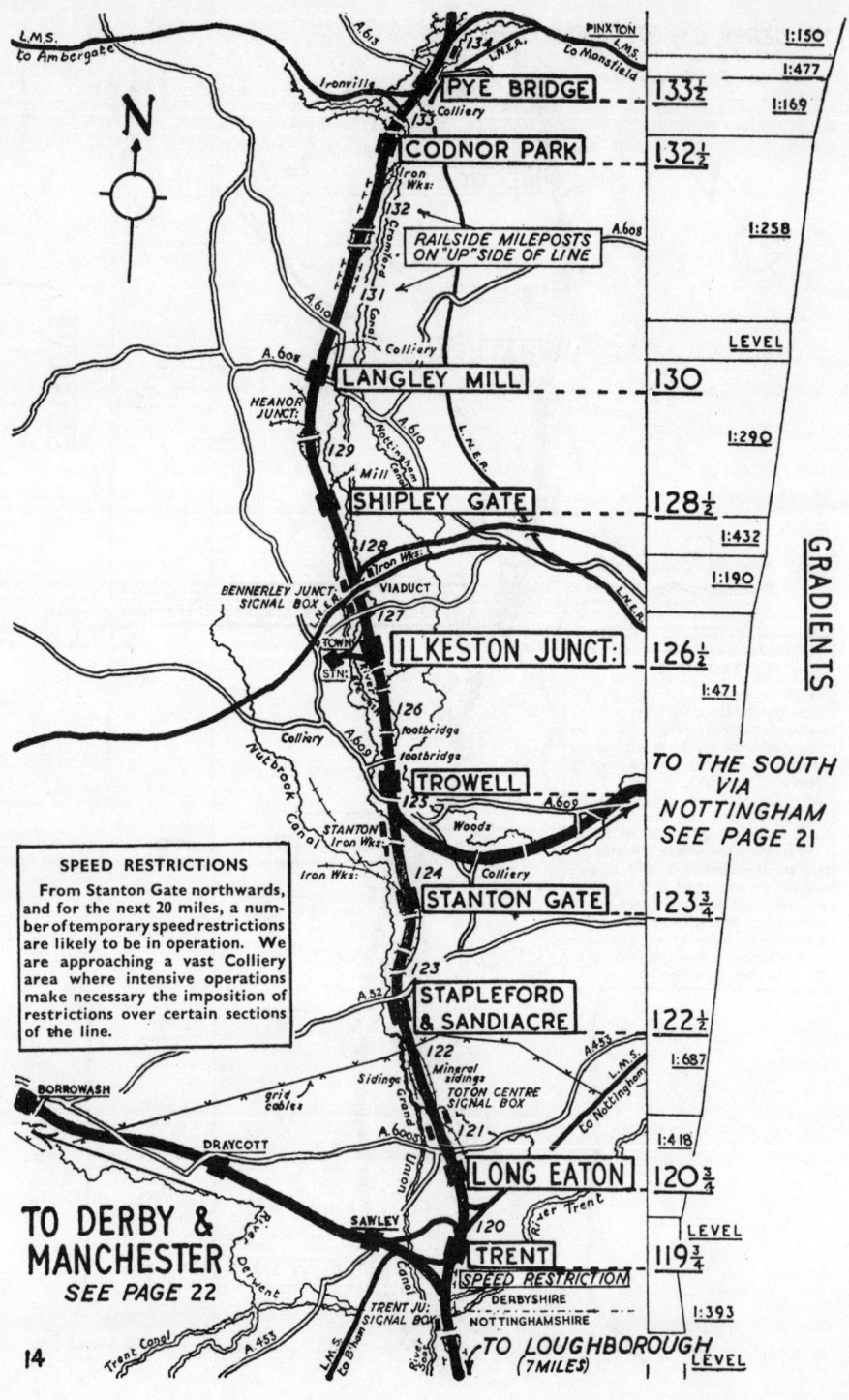

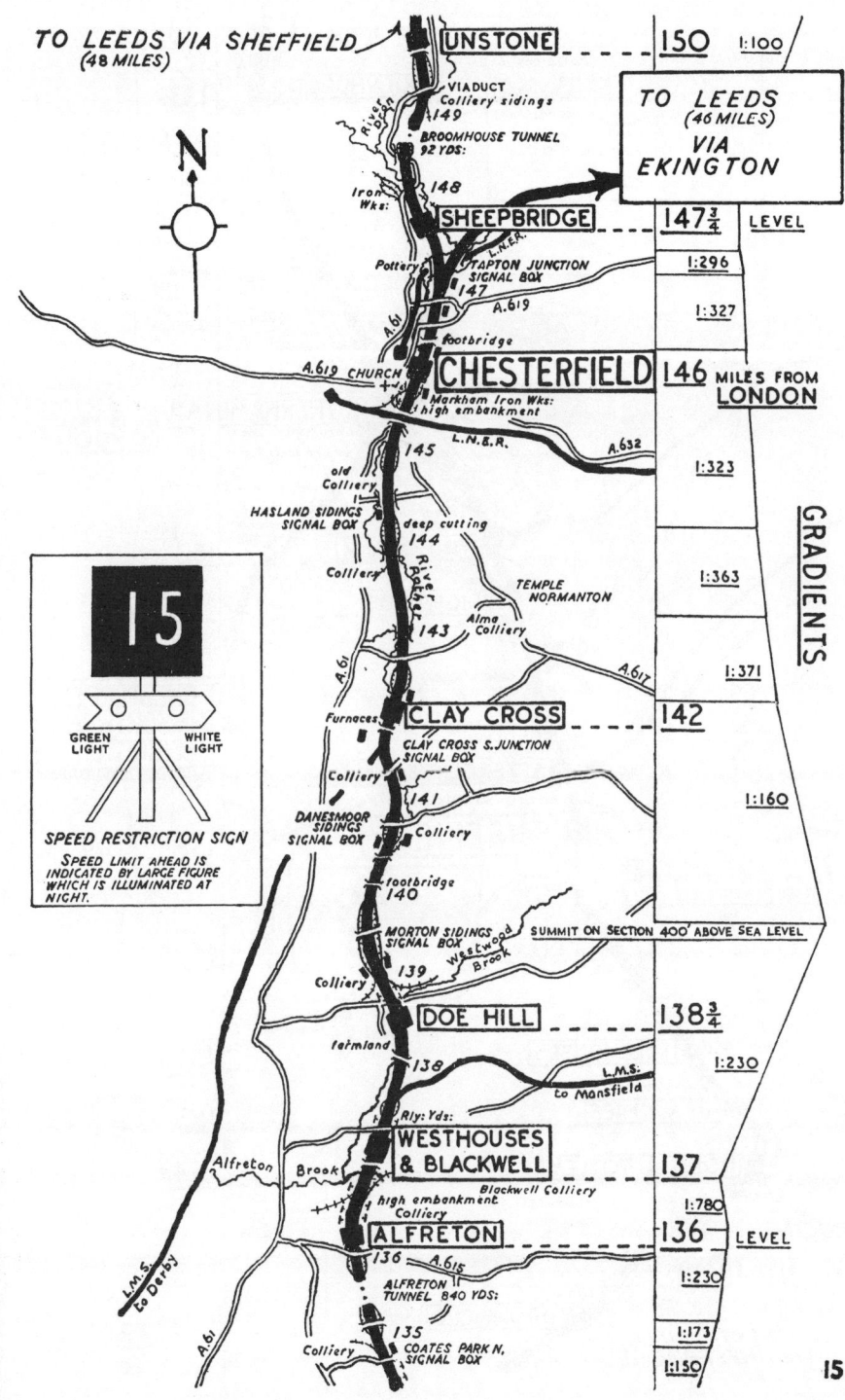

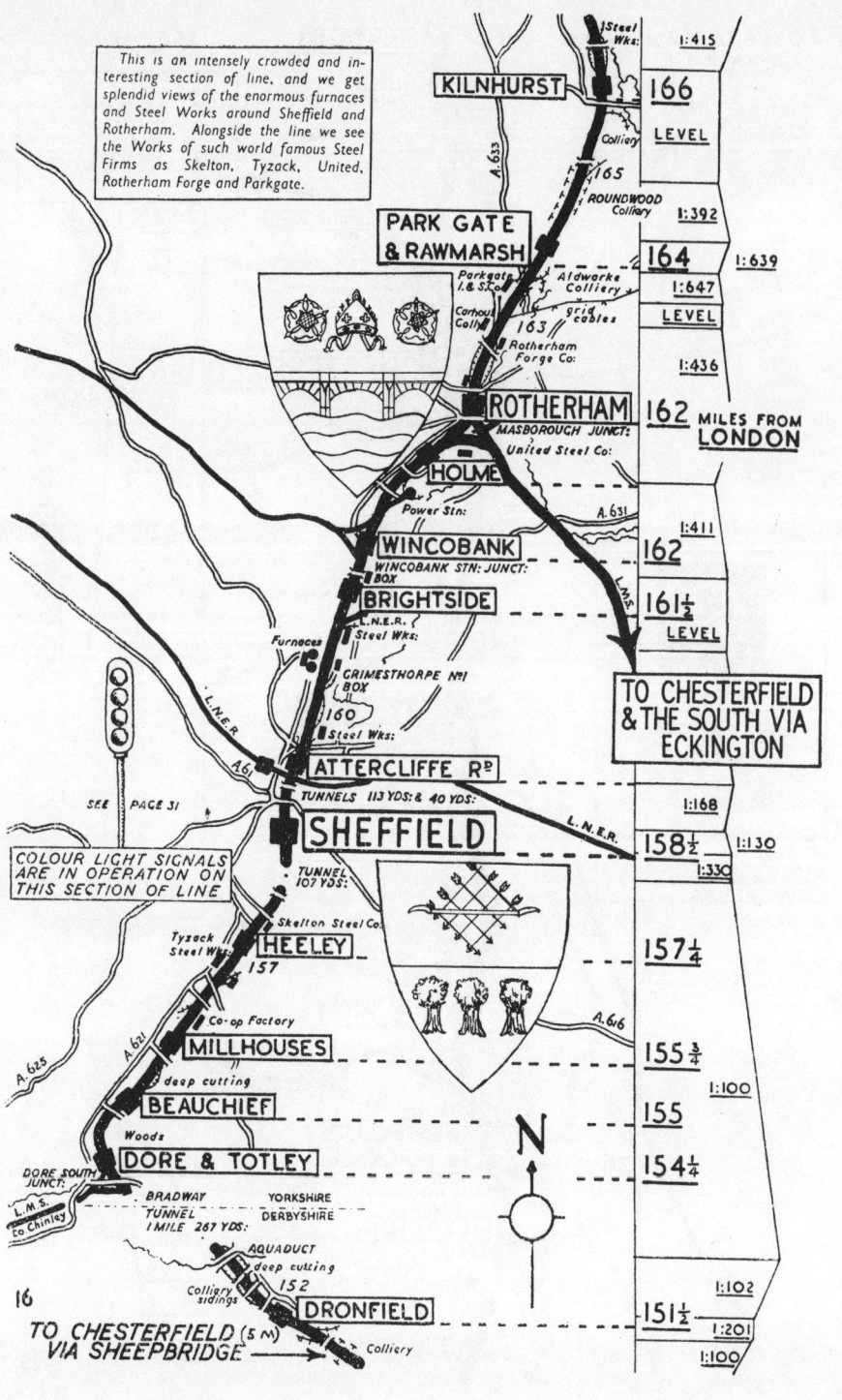

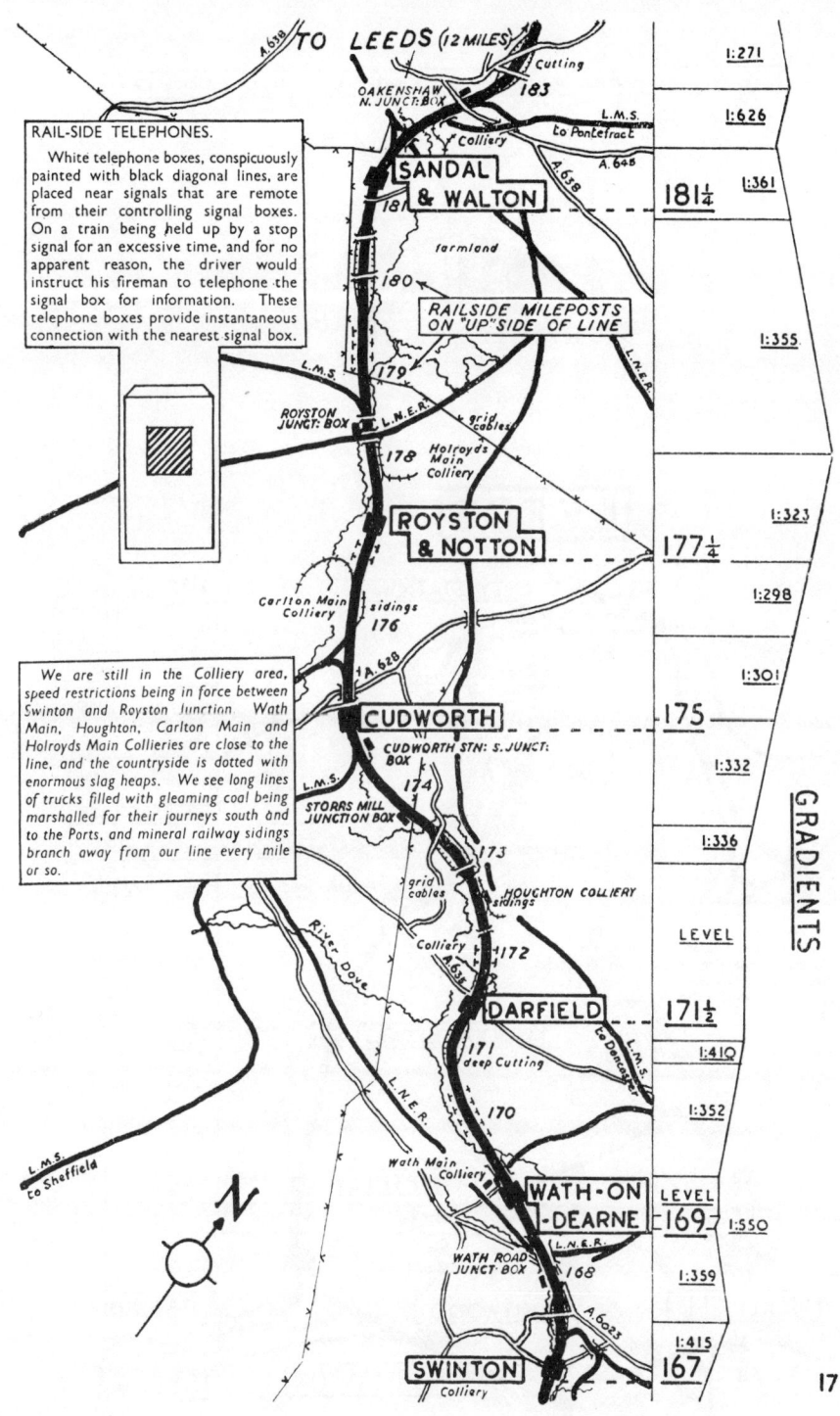

FOR INDEX OF ALL STATIONS, RIVERS, TUNNELS, AND WATER-TROUGH SYSTEMS, SEE PAGES 4, 5, & 6.

LEEDS

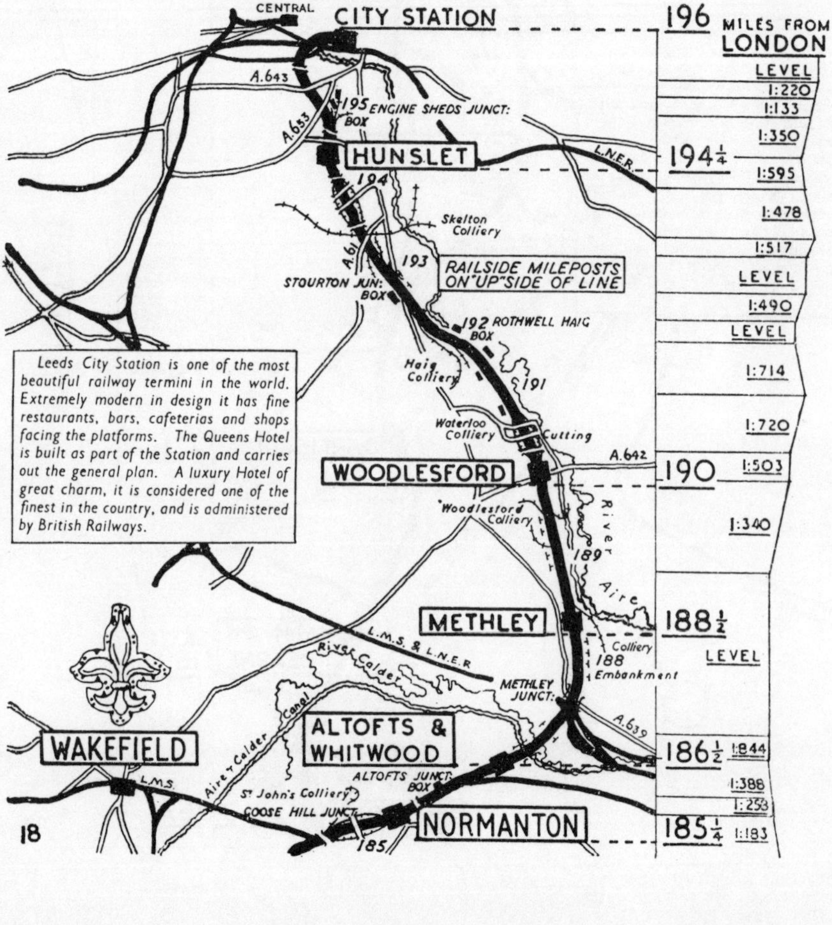

Location	Miles from London	Gradient
CENTRAL CITY STATION	196	LEVEL
		1:220
		1:133
195 ENGINE SHEDS JUNCT. BOX		
HUNSLET	194¼	1:350
194		1:595
Skelton Colliery		1:478
		1:517
STOURTON JUN. BOX 193		LEVEL
RAILSIDE MILEPOSTS ON "UP" SIDE OF LINE		1:490
192 ROTHWELL HAIG BOX		LEVEL
Haig Colliery 191		1:714
Waterloo Colliery Cutting		1:720
WOODLESFORD	190	1:503
Woodlesford Colliery		1:340
189		
METHLEY	188½	LEVEL
188 Colliery Embankment		
METHLEY JUNCT.		
ALTOFTS & WHITWOOD	186½	1:844
ALTOFTS JUNCT BOX		1:388
St John's Colliery GOOSE HILL JUNCT.		1:253
185 NORMANTON	185¼	1:183

WAKEFIELD L.M.S.

Leeds City Station is one of the most beautiful railway termini in the world. Extremely modern in design it has fine restaurants, bars, cafeterias and shops facing the platforms. The Queens Hotel is built as part of the Station and carries out the general plan. A luxury Hotel of great charm, it is considered one of the finest in the country, and is administered by British Railways.

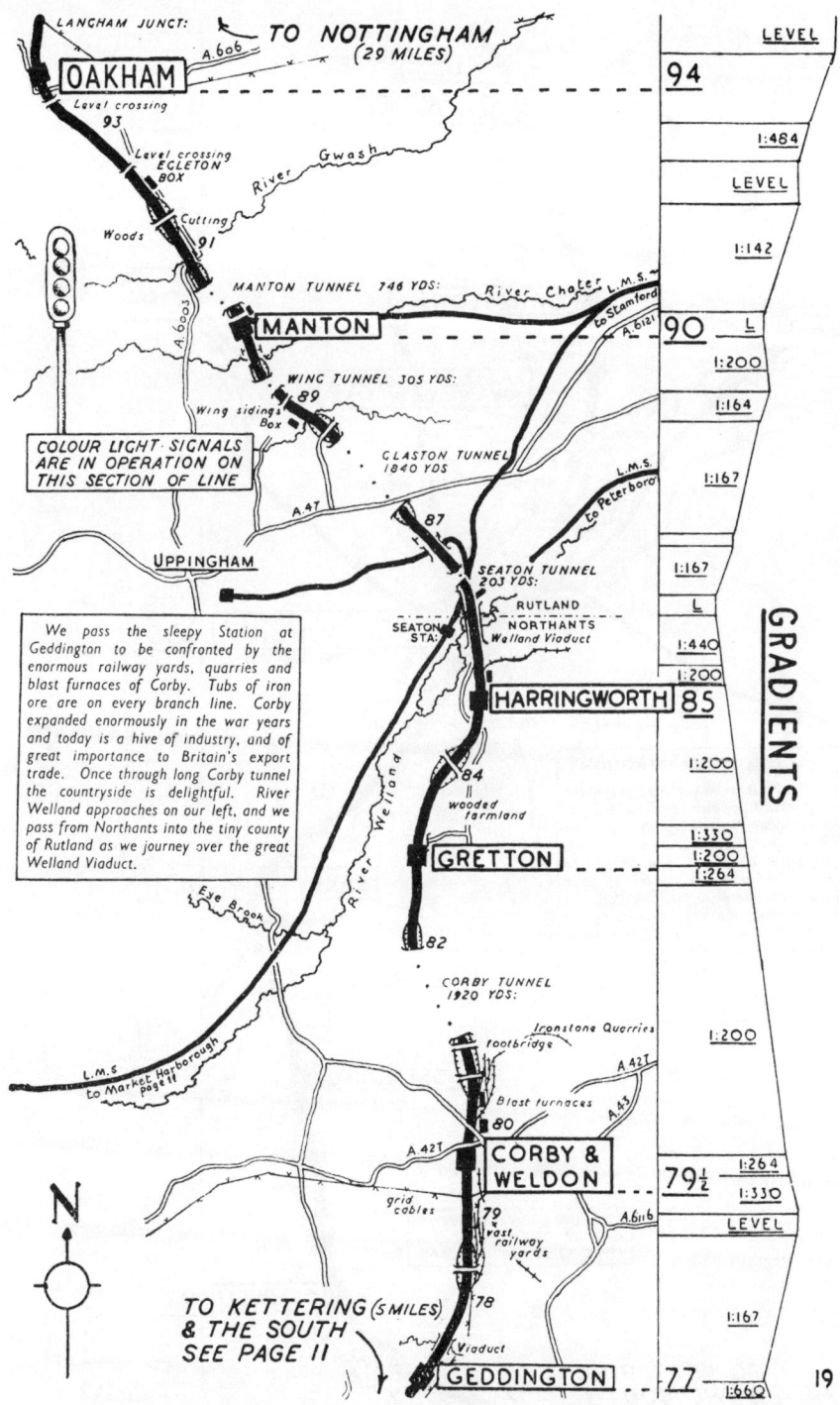

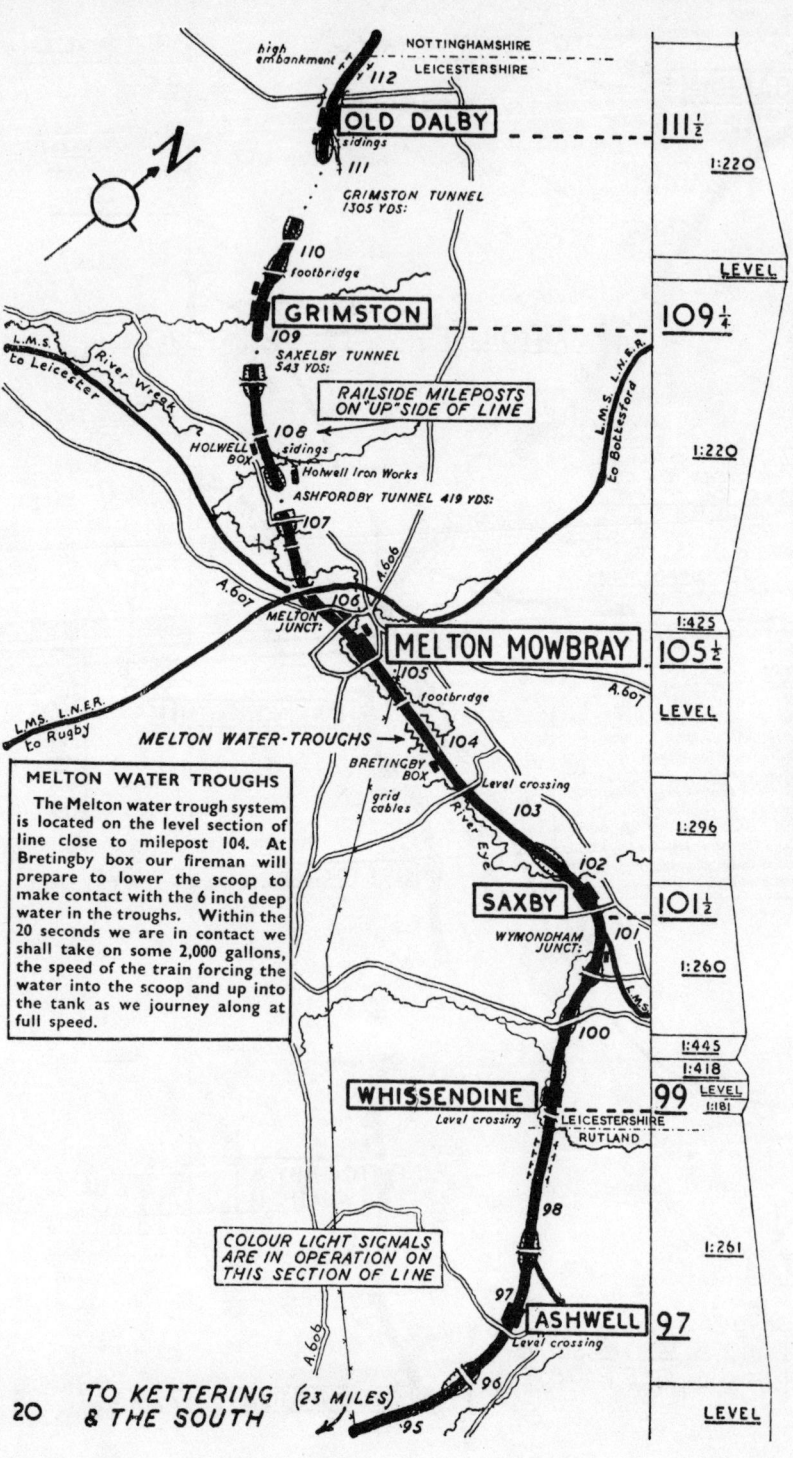

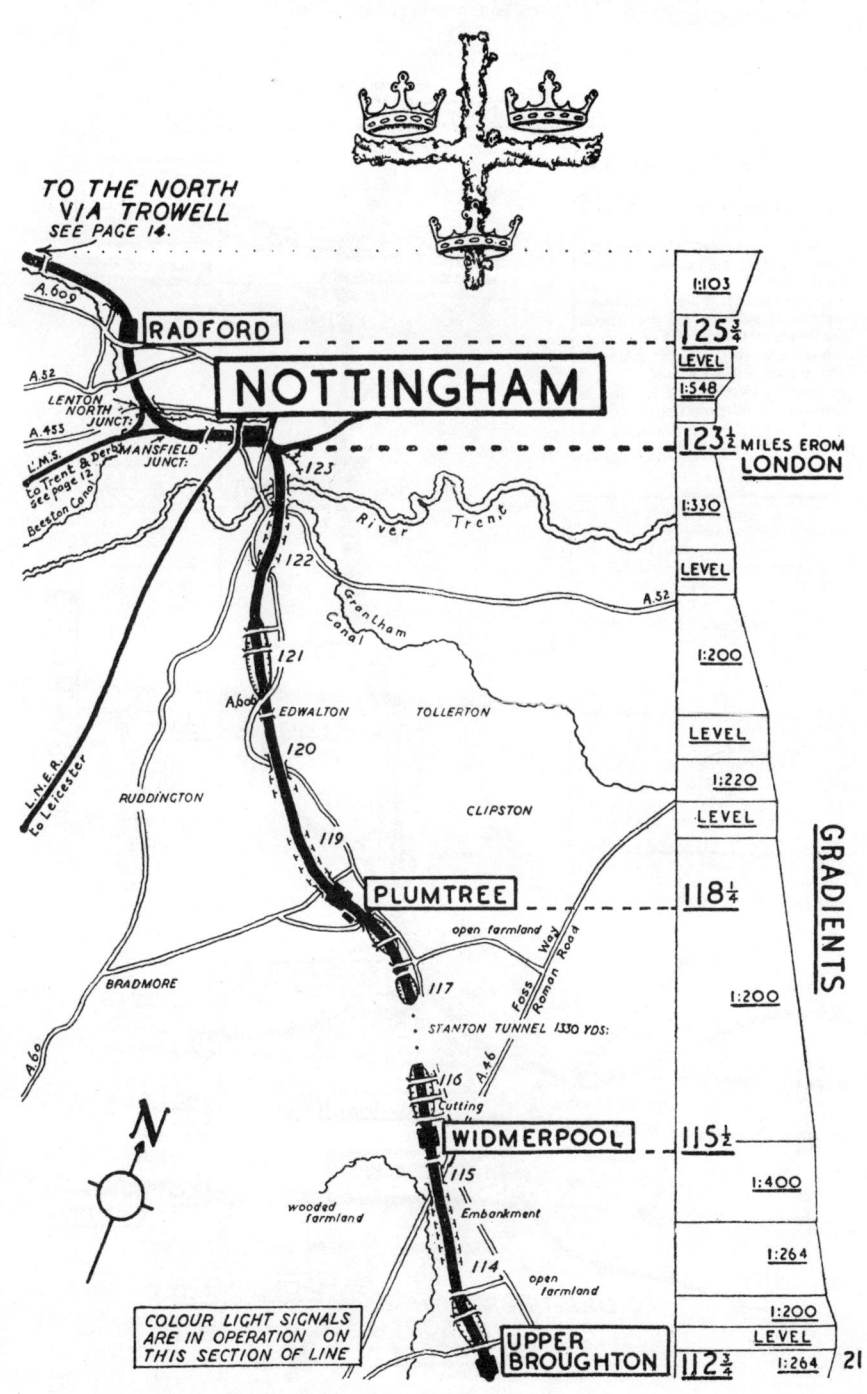

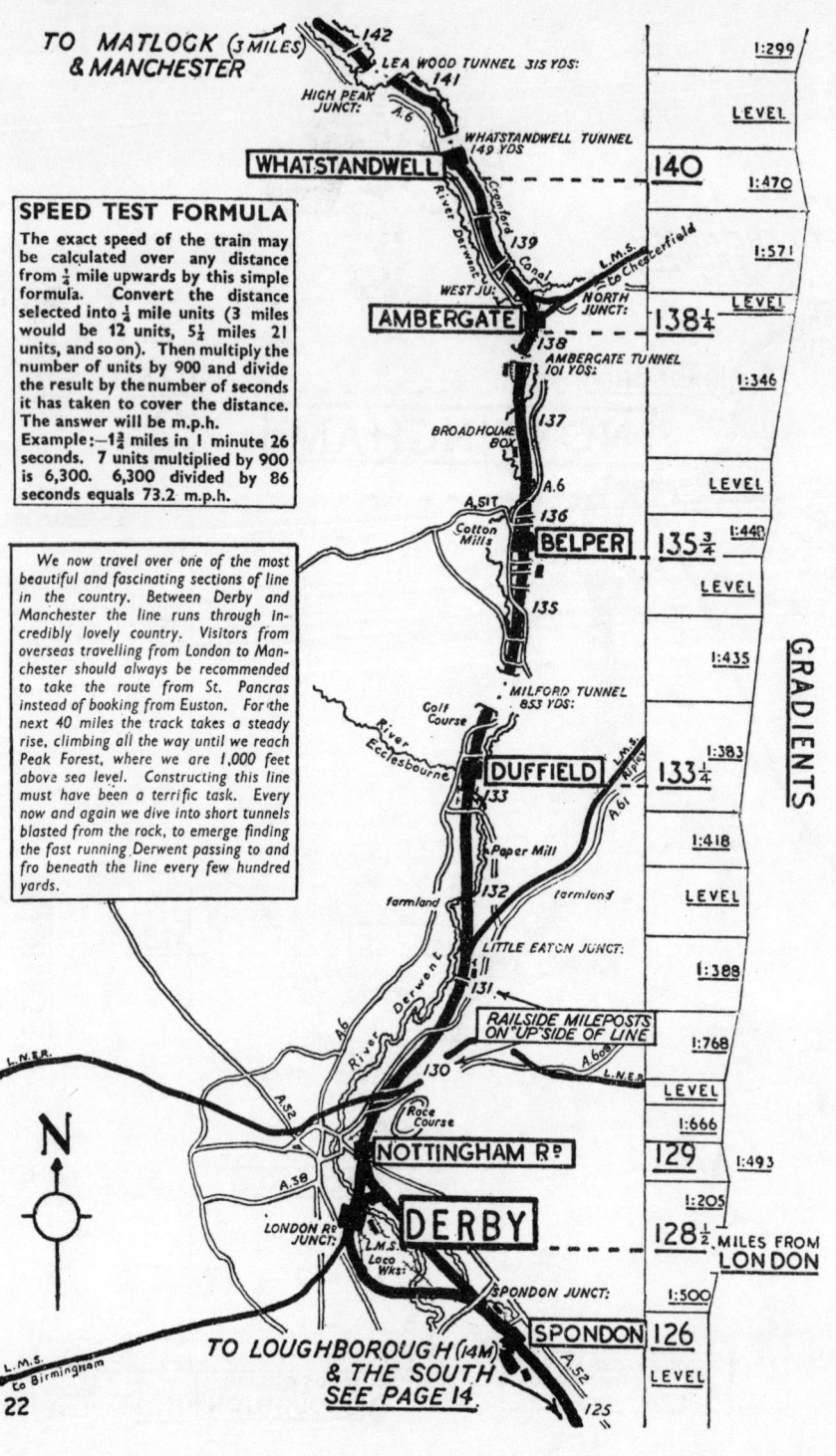

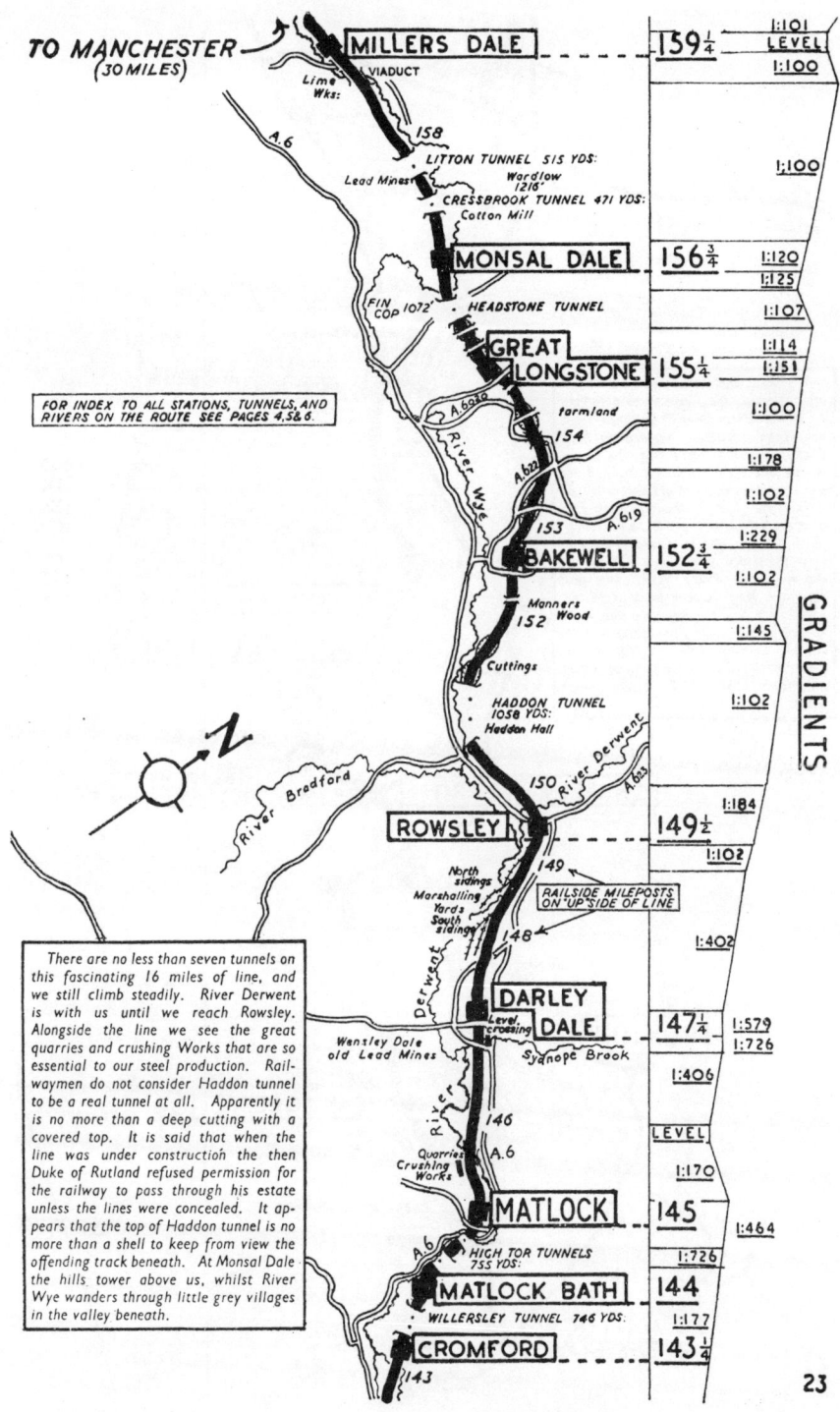

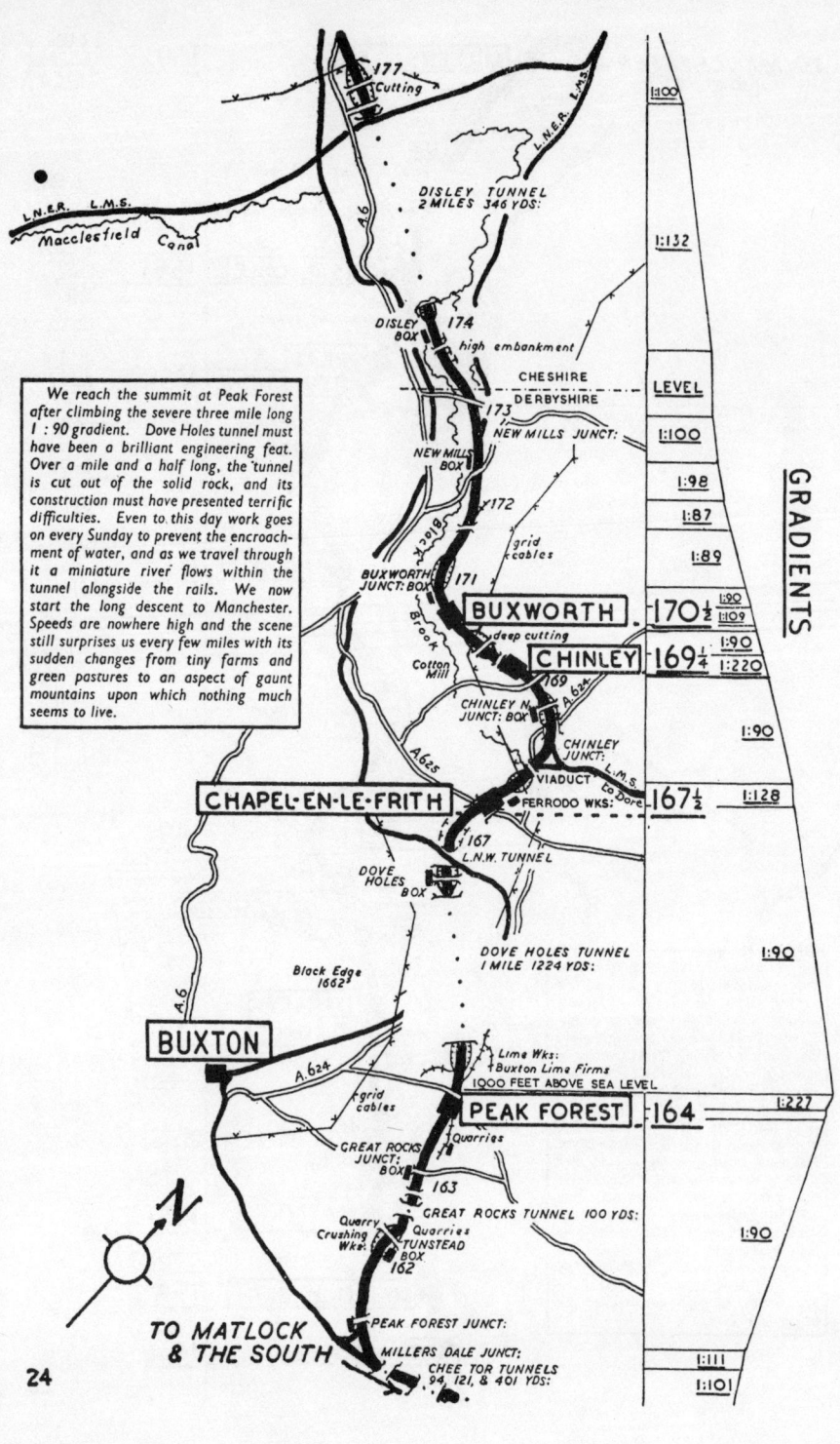

MANCHESTER

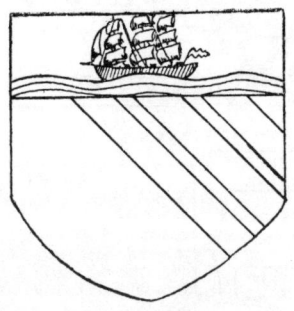

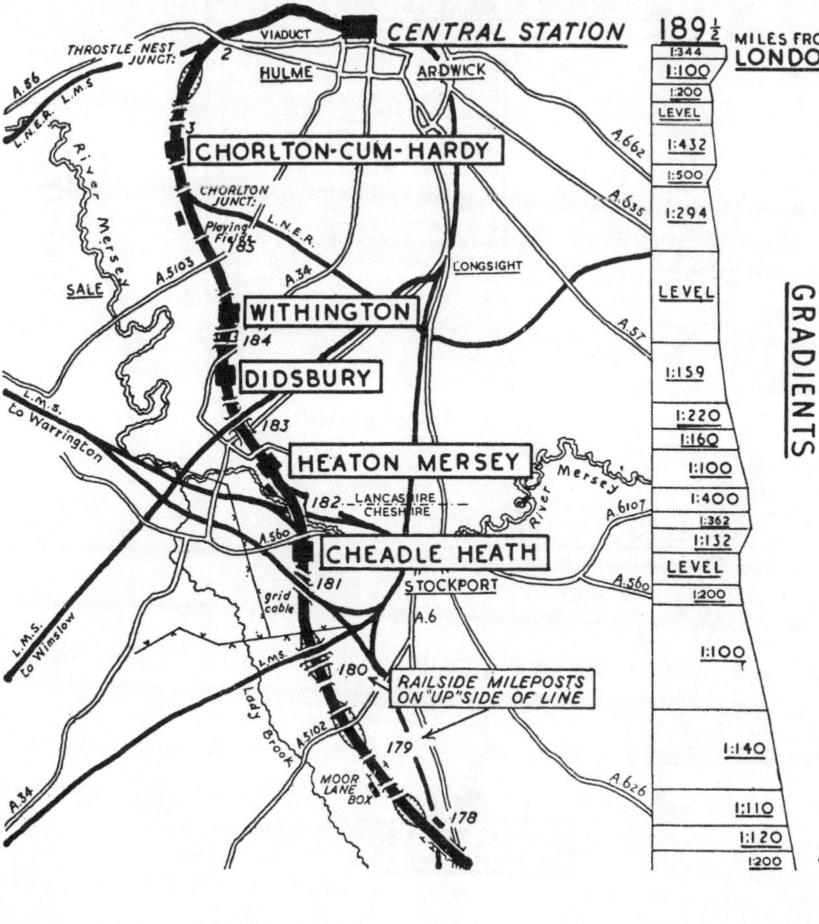

CENTRAL STATION
189½ MILES FROM LONDON
VIADUCT
THROSTLE NEST JUNCT:
HULME
ARDWICK
A.56
L.N.E.R. L.M.S
River Mersey
CHORLTON-CUM-HARDY
CHORLTON JUNCT:
L.N.E.R.
Playing Fields
A.662
A.635
LONGSIGHT
SALE
A.5103
A.34
WITHINGTON
A.57
DIDSBURY
L.M.S. to Warrington
HEATON MERSEY
River Mersey
LANCASHIRE
CHESHIRE
A.6107
A.560
CHEADLE HEATH
STOCKPORT
grid cable
A.6
L.M.S. to Wimslow
L.M.S.
RAILSIDE MILEPOSTS ON "UP" SIDE OF LINE
Lady Brook
A.5102
MOOR LANE BOX
A.626
A.34
2
3
185
184
183
182
181
180
179
178
GRADIENTS
1:344
1:100
1:200
LEVEL
1:432
1:500
1:294
LEVEL
1:159
1:220
1:160
1:100
1:400
1:362
1:132
LEVEL
1:200
1:100
1:140
1:110
1:120
1:200

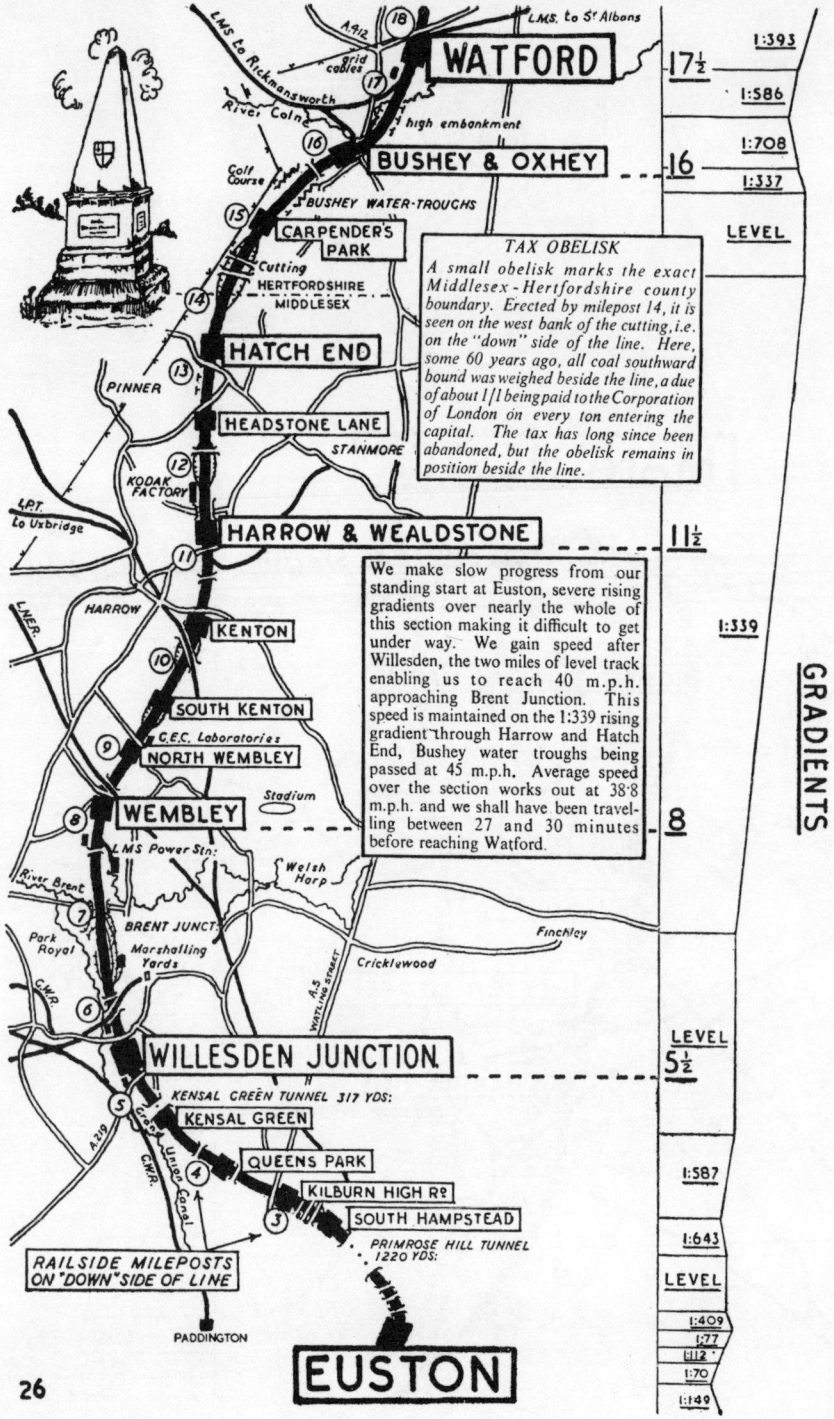

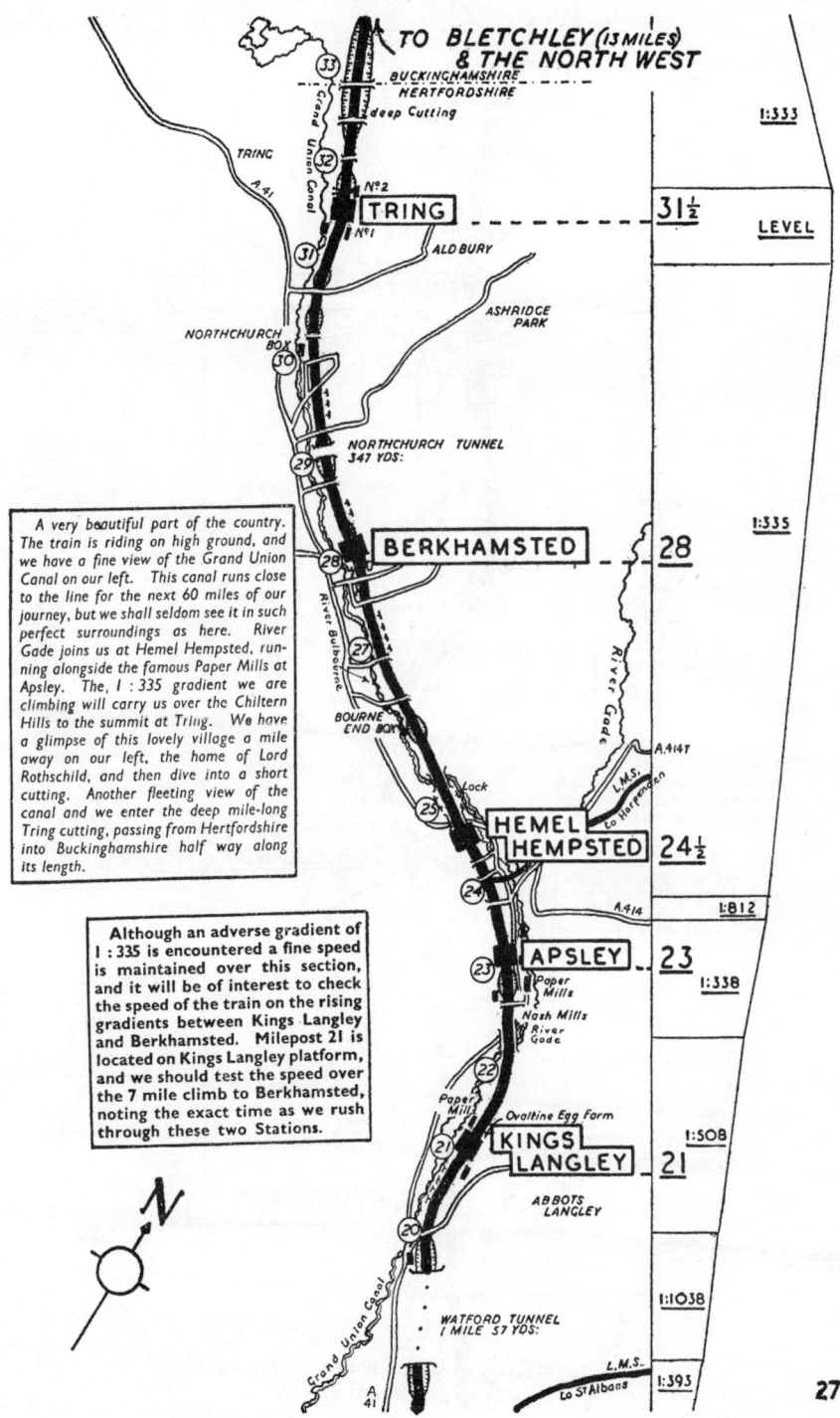

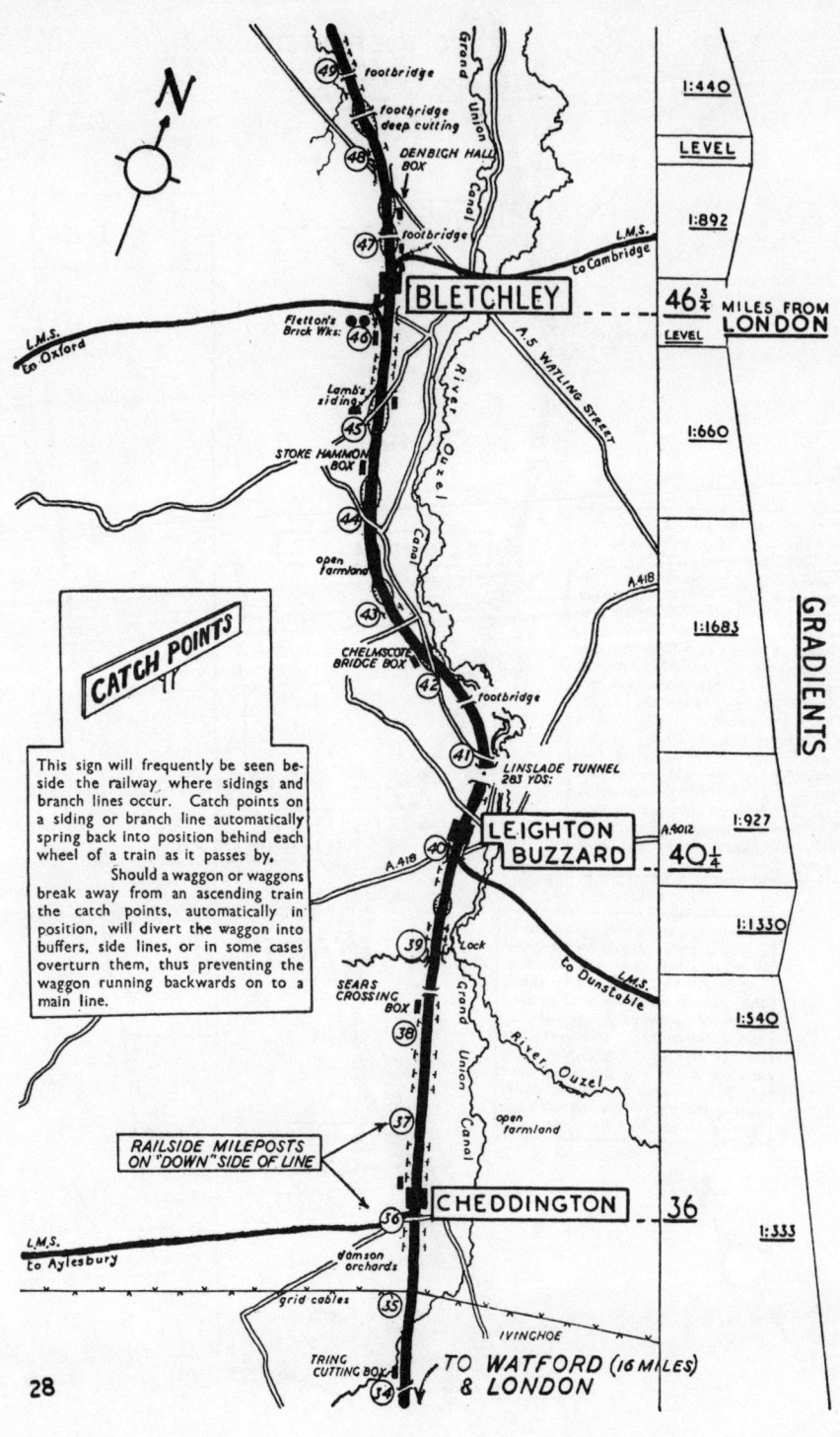

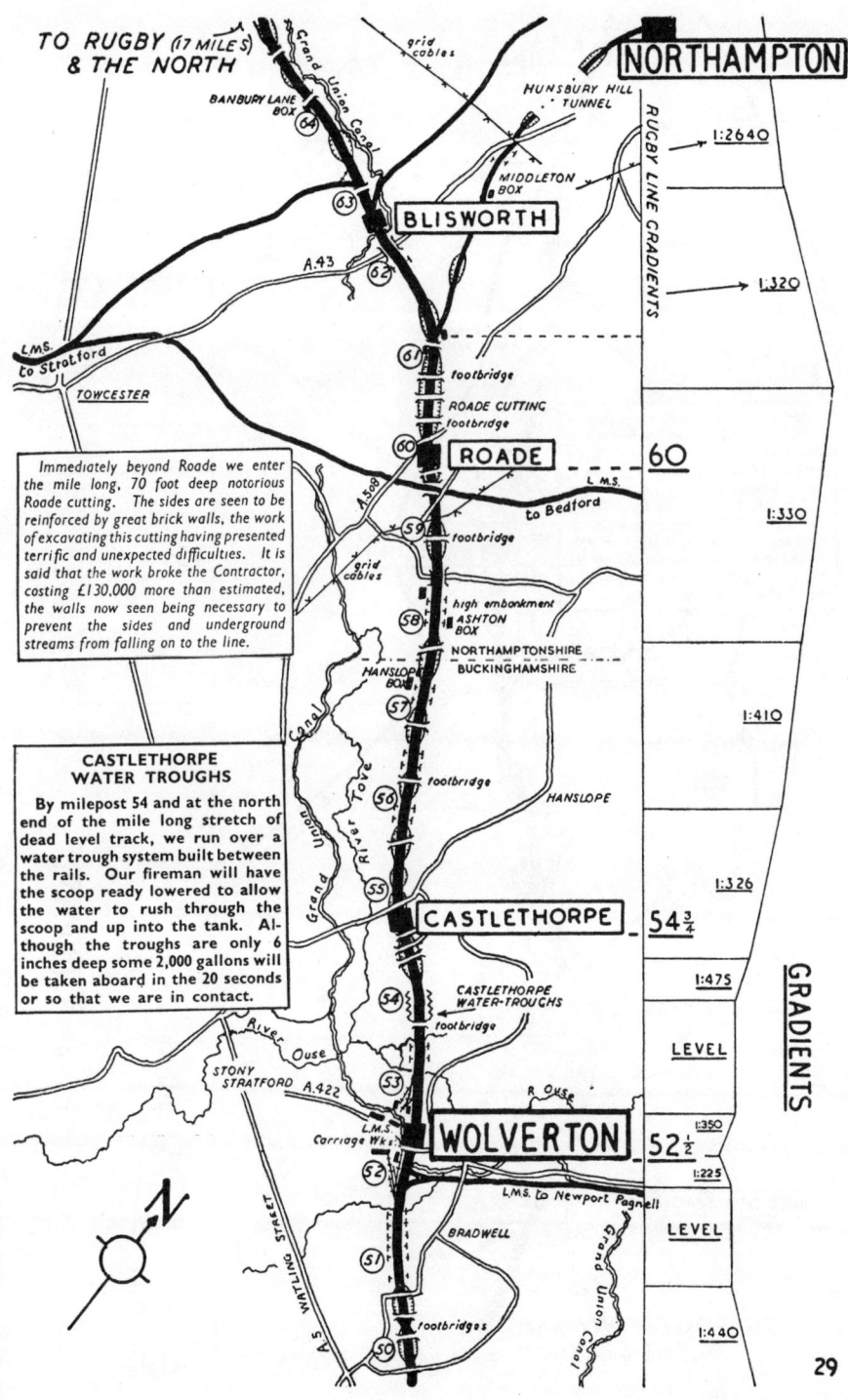

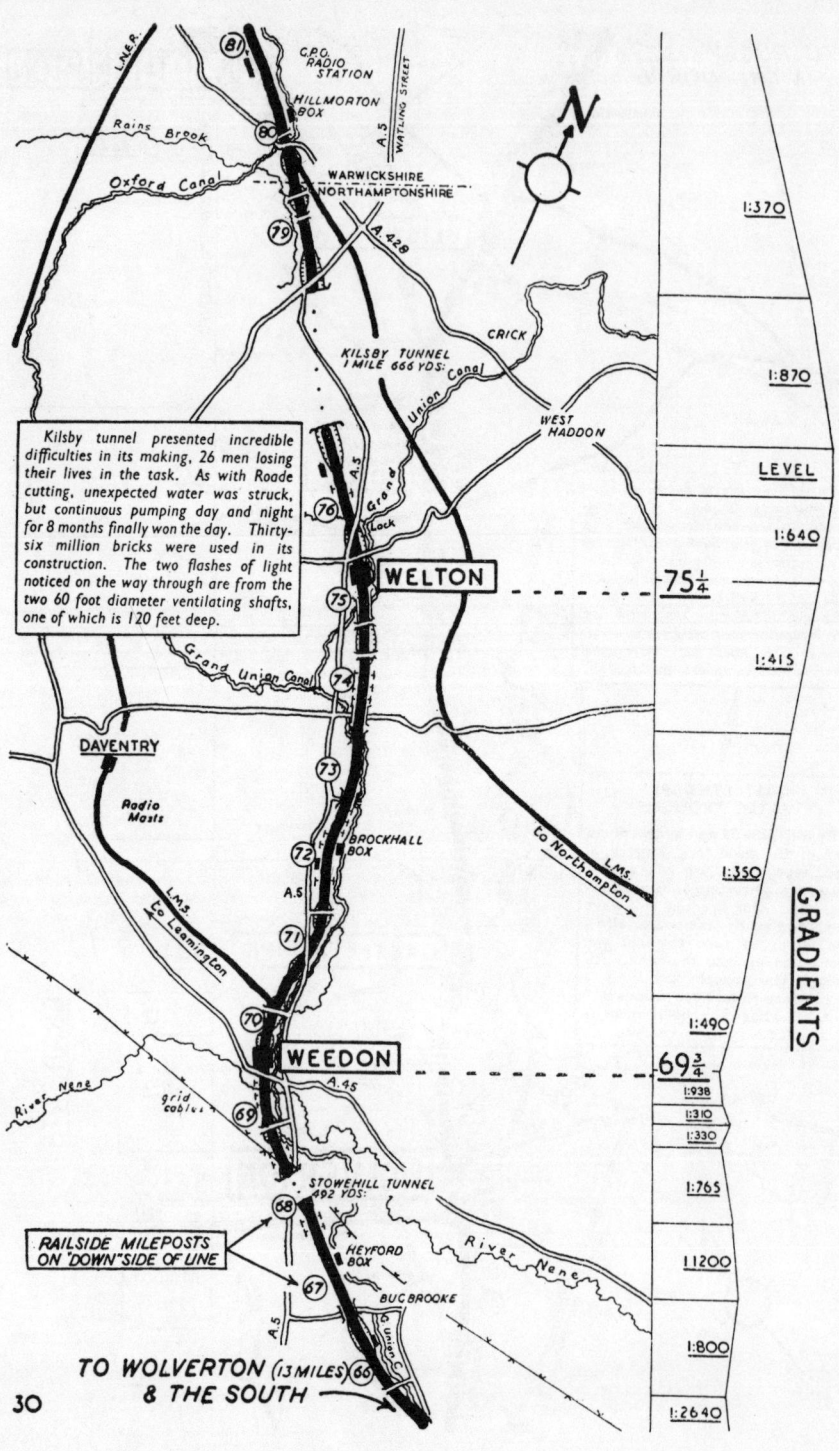

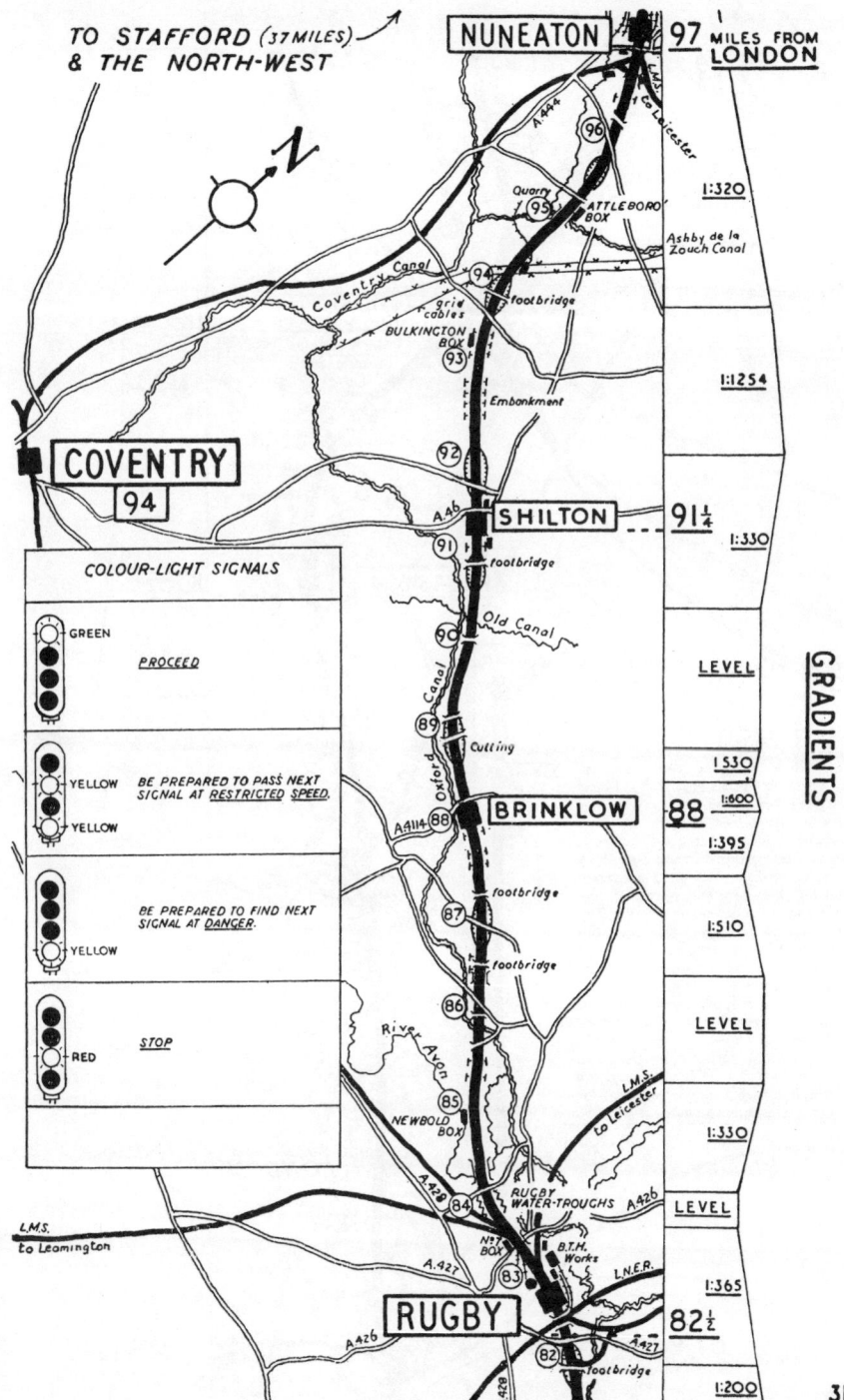

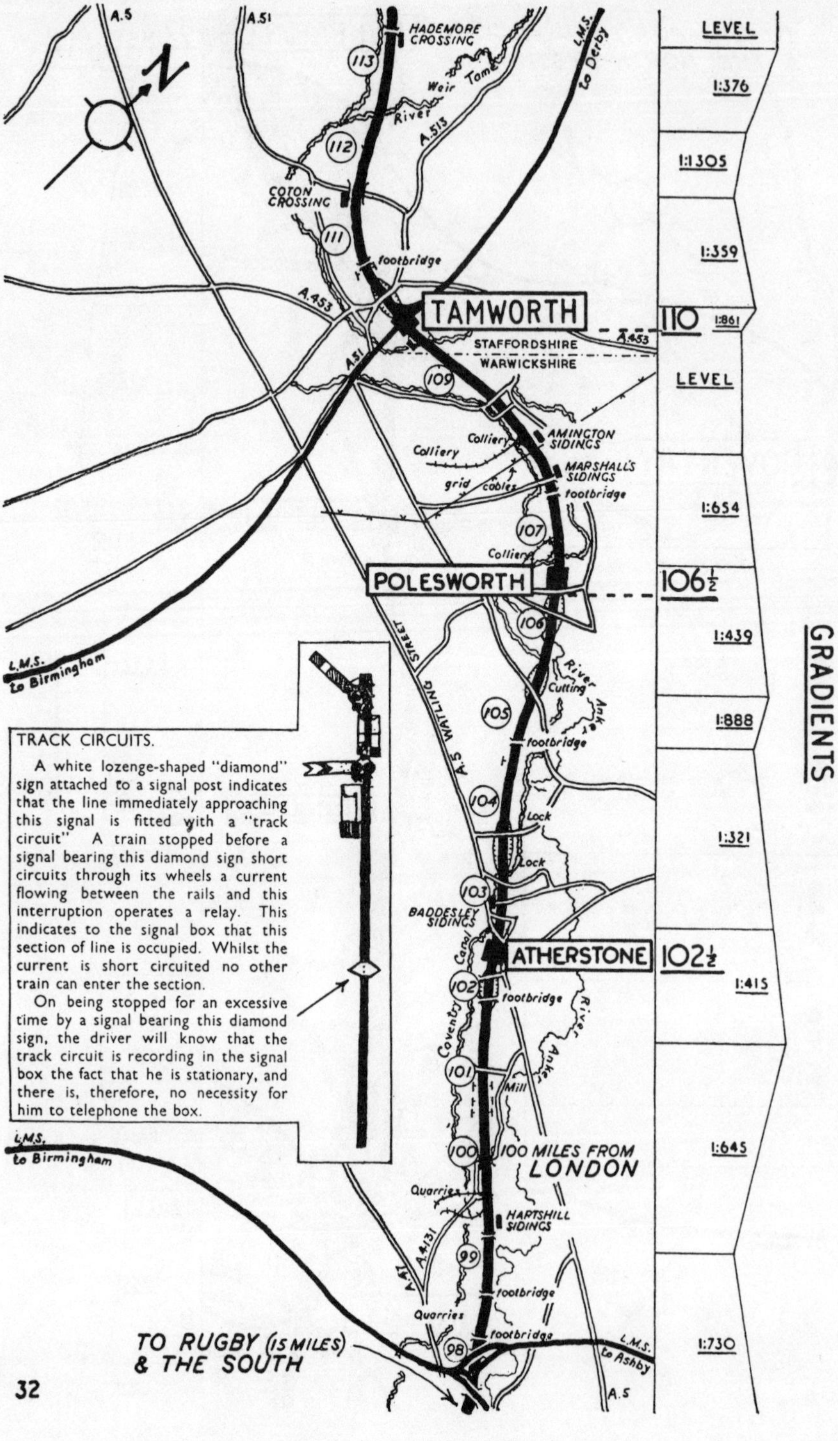

TRACK CIRCUITS.

A white lozenge-shaped "diamond" sign attached to a signal post indicates that the line immediately approaching this signal is fitted with a "track circuit." A train stopped before a signal bearing this diamond sign short circuits through its wheels a current flowing between the rails and this interruption operates a relay. This indicates to the signal box that this section of line is occupied. Whilst the current is short circuited no other train can enter the section.

On being stopped for an excessive time by a signal bearing this diamond sign, the driver will know that the track circuit is recording in the signal box the fact that he is stationary, and there is, therefore, no necessity for him to telephone the box.

GRADIENTS

| LEVEL |
| 1:376 |
| 1:1305 |
| 1:359 |
| 110 1:861 |
| LEVEL |
| 1:654 |
| 106½ 1:439 |
| 1:888 |
| 1:321 |
| 102½ 1:415 |
| 1:645 |
| 1:730 |

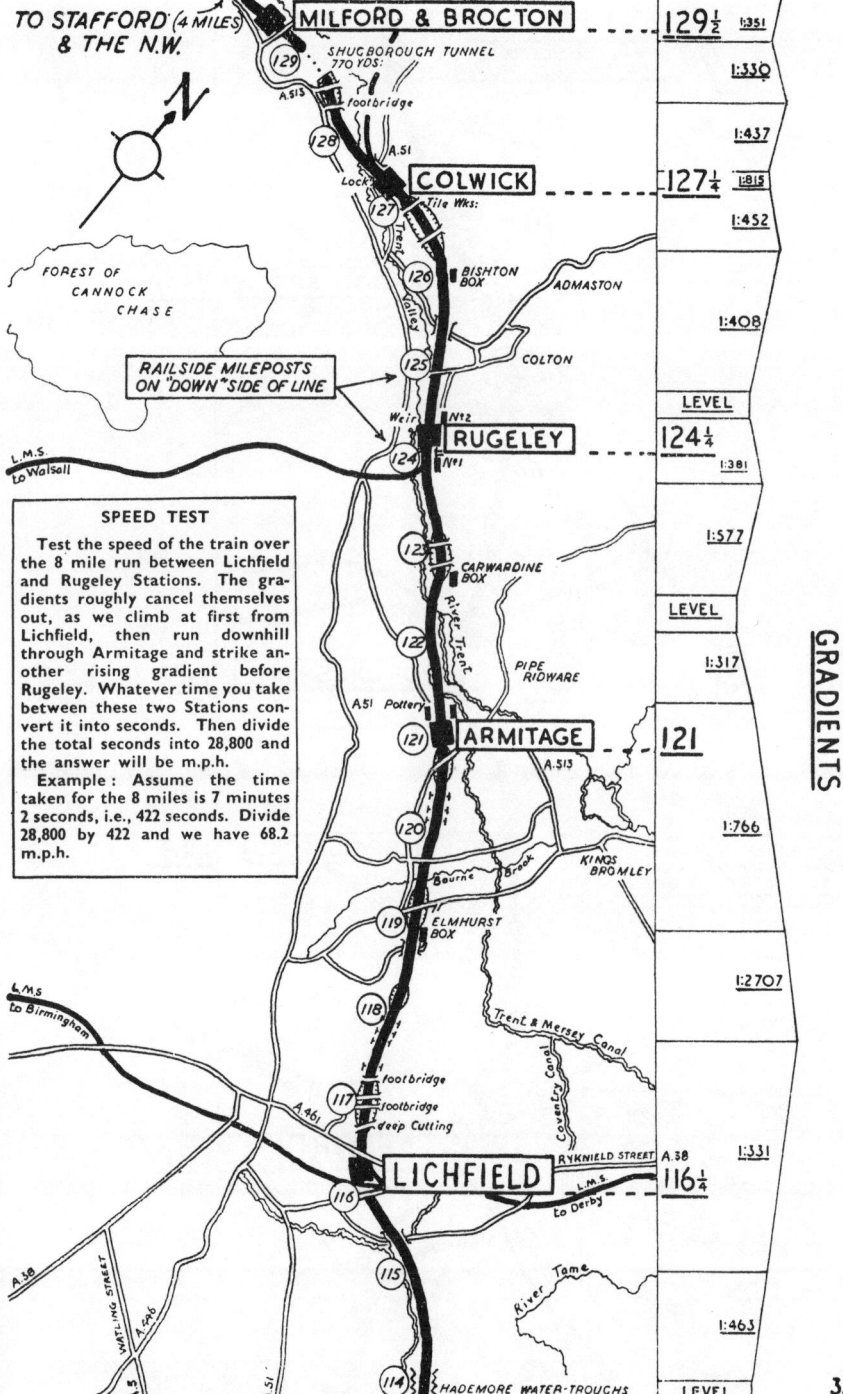

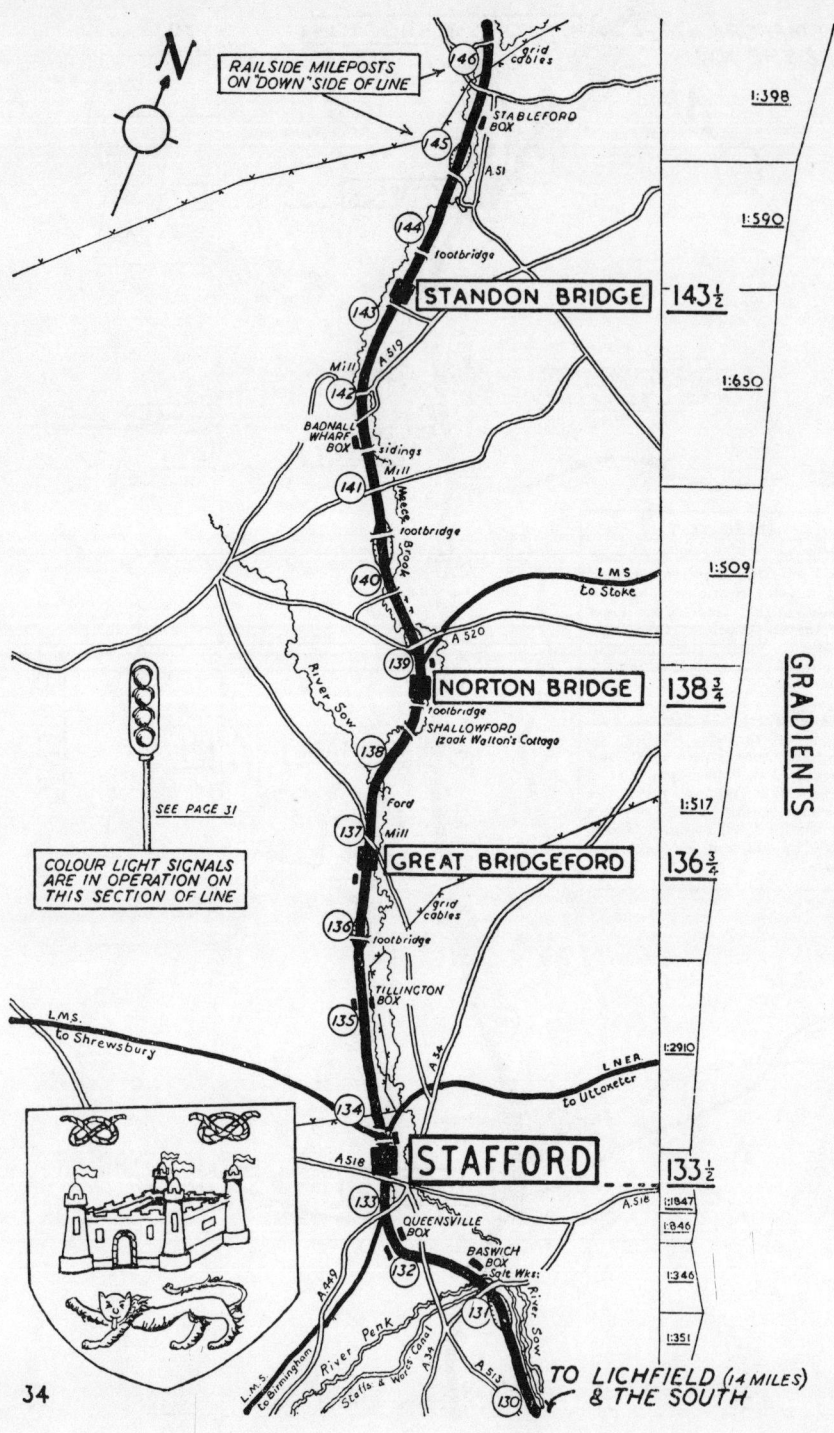

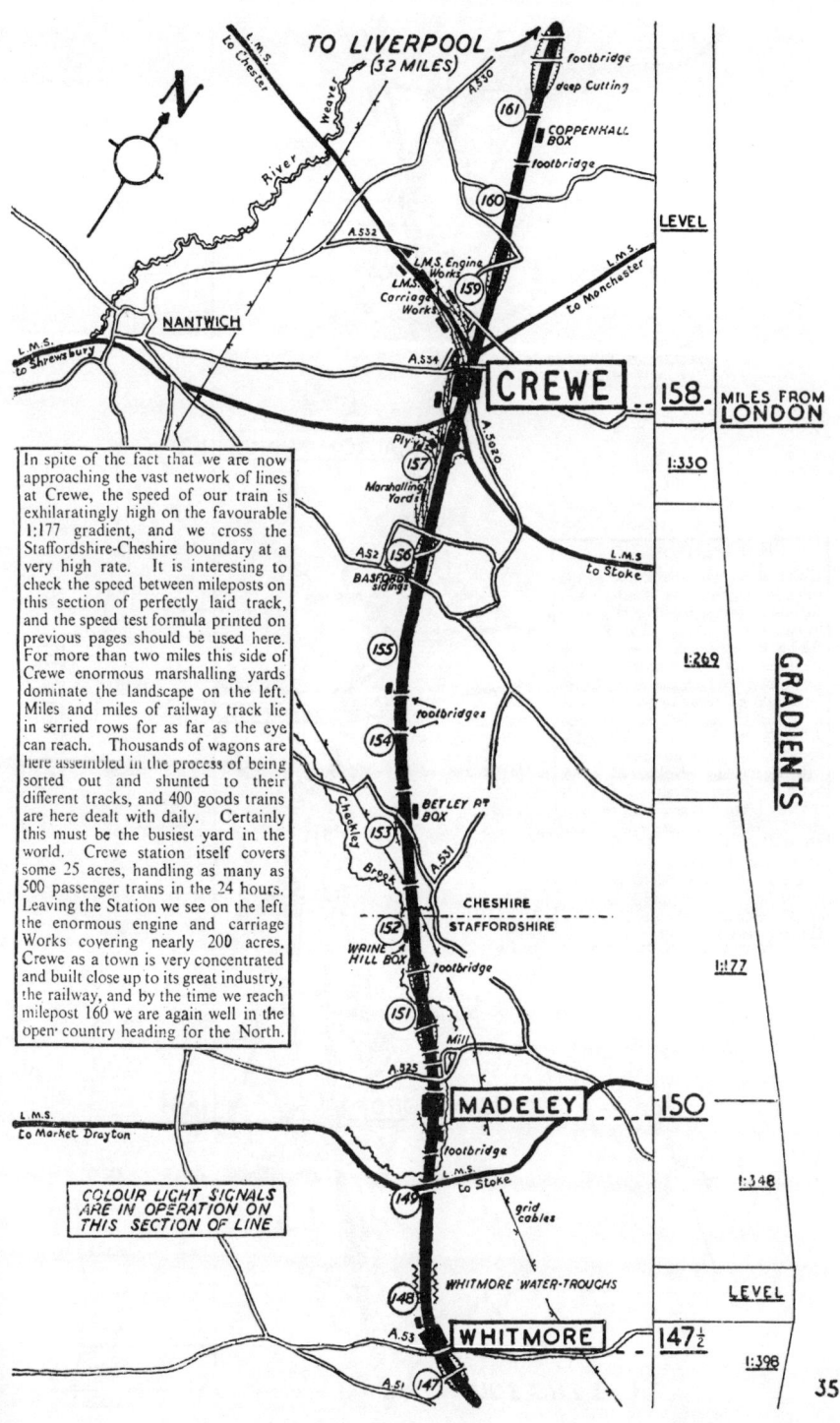

In spite of the fact that we are now approaching the vast network of lines at Crewe, the speed of our train is exhilaratingly high on the favourable 1:177 gradient, and we cross the Staffordshire-Cheshire boundary at a very high rate. It is interesting to check the speed between mileposts on this section of perfectly laid track, and the speed test formula printed on previous pages should be used here. For more than two miles this side of Crewe enormous marshalling yards dominate the landscape on the left. Miles and miles of railway track lie in serried rows for as far as the eye can reach. Thousands of wagons are here assembled in the process of being sorted out and shunted to their different tracks, and 400 goods trains are here dealt with daily. Certainly this must be the busiest yard in the world. Crewe station itself covers some 25 acres, handling as many as 500 passenger trains in the 24 hours. Leaving the Station we see on the left the enormous engine and carriage Works covering nearly 200 acres. Crewe as a town is very concentrated and built close up to its great industry, the railway, and by the time we reach milepost 160 we are again well in the open country heading for the North.

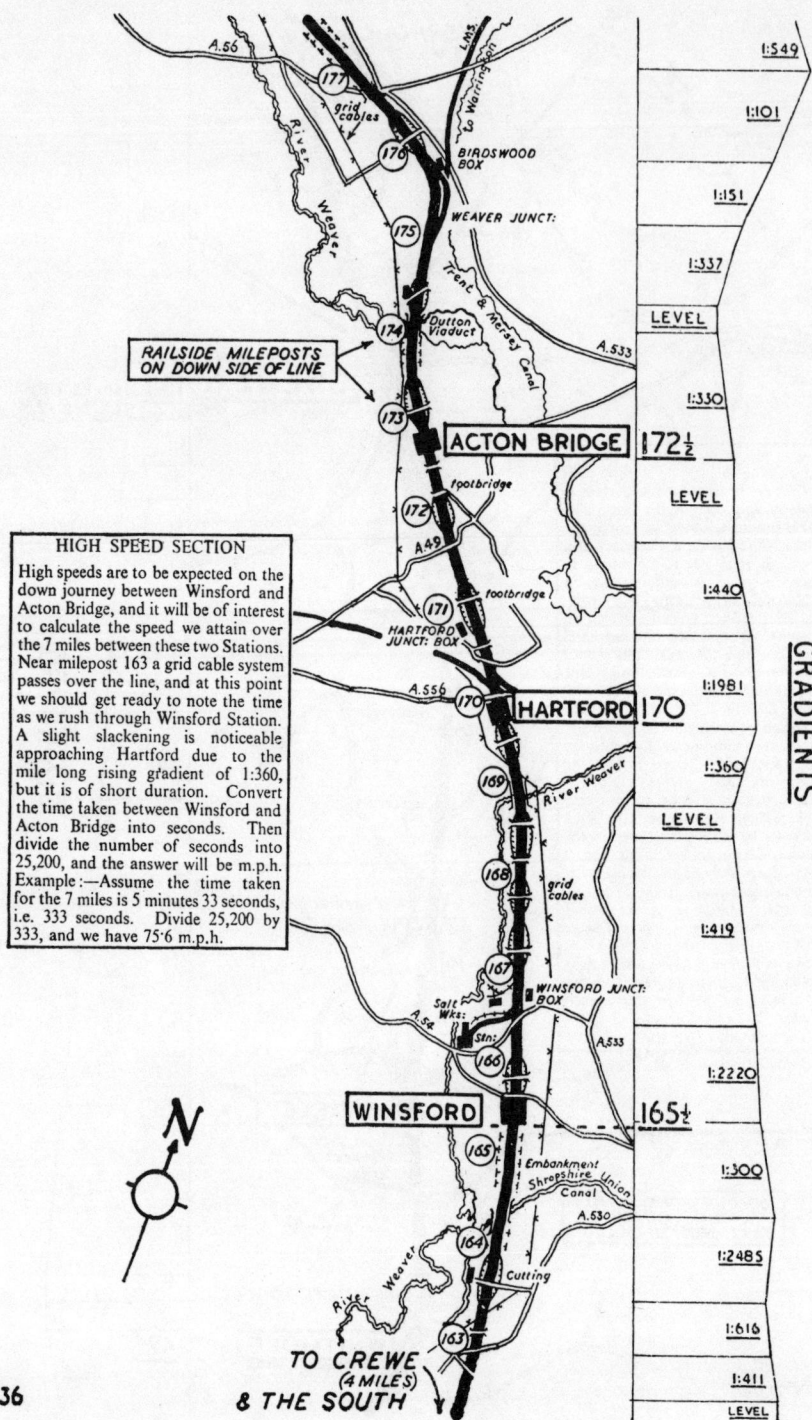

HIGH SPEED SECTION

High speeds are to be expected on the down journey between Winsford and Acton Bridge, and it will be of interest to calculate the speed we attain over the 7 miles between these two Stations. Near milepost 163 a grid cable system passes over the line, and at this point we should get ready to note the time as we rush through Winsford Station. A slight slackening is noticeable approaching Hartford due to the mile long rising gradient of 1:360, but it is of short duration. Convert the time taken between Winsford and Acton Bridge into seconds. Then divide the number of seconds into 25,200, and the answer will be m.p.h. Example:—Assume the time taken for the 7 miles is 5 minutes 33 seconds, i.e. 333 seconds. Divide 25,200 by 333, and we have 75·6 m.p.h.

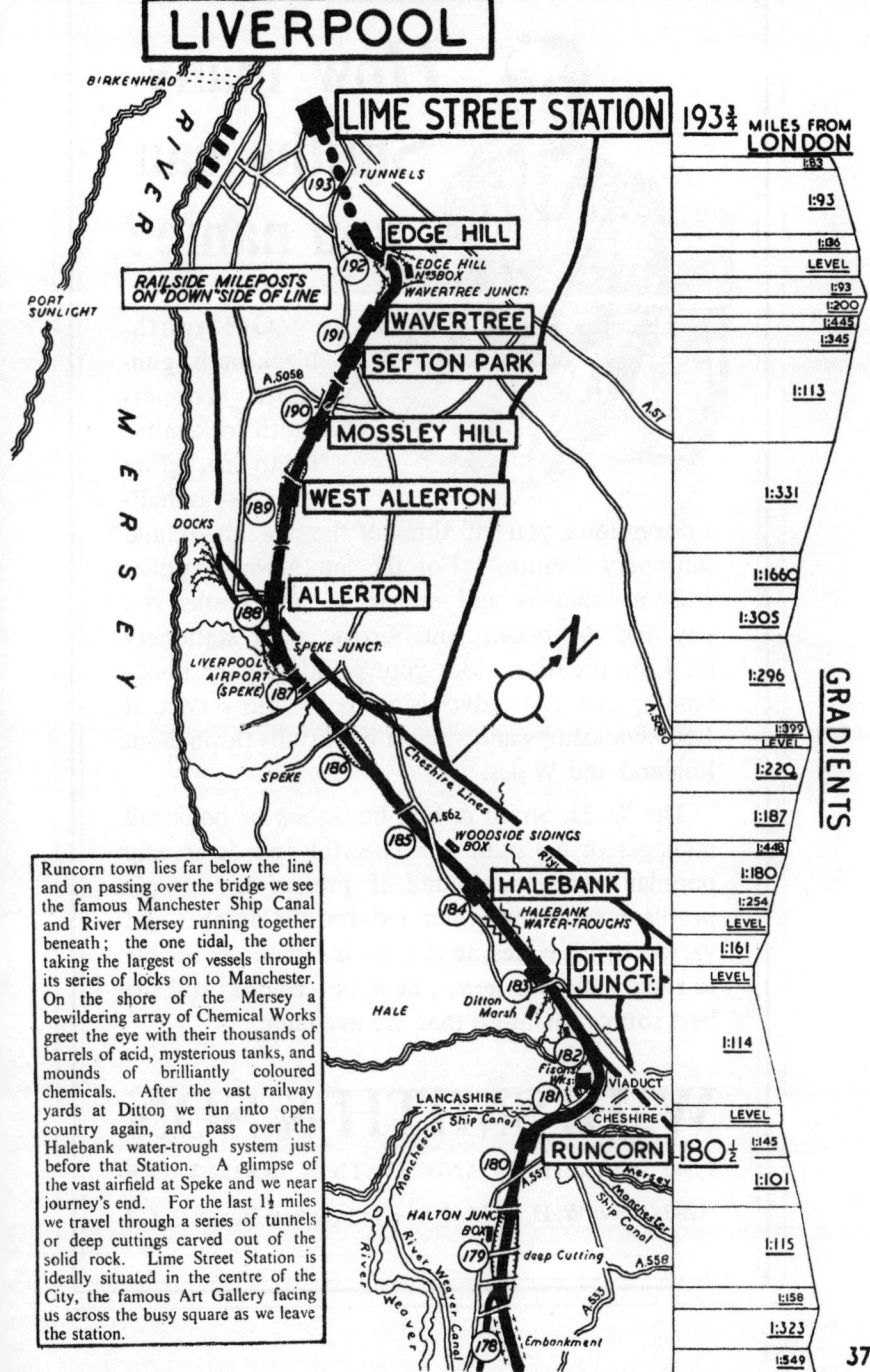

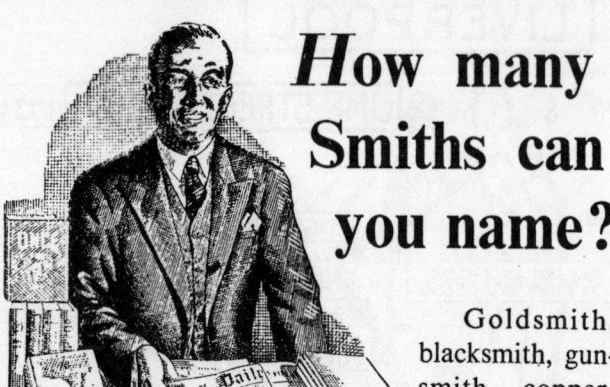

How many Smiths can you name?

Goldsmith, blacksmith, gunsmith, coppersmith, locksmith: ten to one, before your list is half-a-dozen long, you will think of the news, book and stationery "Smith." For the Smith who supplies your newspapers and magazines, the books you buy and the books you borrow, your stationery (and, on occasion, does your printing, your bookbinding and your advertising) is at your service at 1,500 bookshops and station bookstalls throughout England and Wales.

The W. H. Smith & Son bookshop or bookstall manager or assistant is a cheerful and deservedly popular personality; and if present-day supply problems have somewhat reduced the number and variety of his wares, so that he is sometimes unable to supply all your needs, he is nevertheless still the best source for those that are available.

W. H. SMITH & SON
1,500 BOOKSHOPS AND STATION BOOKSTALLS
Head Office: W. H. Smith & Son, Ltd., Strand House, W.C.2

How are things at
HOME?

All's well, no doubt—but, more than ever when you are away, what a comfort it is to feel that contingencies are covered by a sound insurance policy. Yes, it's very reassuring to have a policy like the 'General's' Householders' Comprehensive Policy, which gives you cover against the losses and liabilities every householder faces. Find out more about this policy and its valuable 'six years' insurance for five premiums' concession. Write to:

GENERAL
Accident Fire & Life Assurance Corporation Ltd.

★

Chief Offices:
GENERAL BUILDINGS, PERTH, SCOTLAND
GENERAL BUILDINGS, ALDWYCH, LONDON, W.C.2

HC5

This is the way to
RHEUMATIC RELIEF

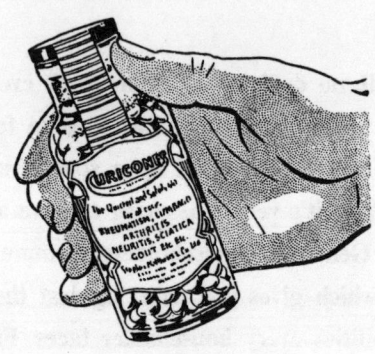

'Curicones' have proved a turning point in the life of many a Rheumatic sufferer. This great treatment has brought freedom from the cruel pains of Rheumatism, Gout, Lumbago, Sciatica, Neuritis, Synovitis, Fibrositis, Swollen Joints, and kindred ills. The large volume of testimony, accumulated over years, is ample tribute to the power of 'CURICONES.' Such testimony cannot be denied. **It is your assurance of the substantial relief that 'Curicones' have brought to others.** All ingredients in 'Curicones' are fully approved by the British Pharmaceutical Authoritiies. Begin a course of 'Curicones' today.

FROM ALL CHEMISTS